Prince and the Paupers

The Companion Volume to Prohibition's Prince

by

Guy Graybill

Foreword by presidential speech-writer James Humes

PRINCE AND THE PAUPERS

THE COMPANION VOLUME TO Prohibition's Prince

FIRST SUNBURY PRESS EDITION
Printed in the United States of America
October 2011

ISBN 978-1-934597-79-8

Published by:
Sunbury Press, Inc.
2200 Market Street
Camp Hill, PA   17011

www.sunburypress.com

Camp Hill, Pennsylvania   USA

Books by Guy Graybill:

Keystone, 2004

BRAVO!, 2008

Prohibition's Prince, 2010

Prince and the Paupers, 2011

Front cover: Depicted here are four friends of Prince Farrington: From left: "Pud" Hill, Lemuel Groce, Charl Farrington and Colonel Segraves.

DEDICATION

This book tells of intemperance and disregard for society that appeared during the nation's Prohibition Era (1919-1933). The setting for this biography is Clinton and Lycoming counties in Pennsylvania.

As the last paragraphs of this book were being written, residents of that same area were pleasantly distracted by a group of eleven young men, and their adult mentors, who showed us what can be accomplished by healthy habits, determination and natural ability. Here we list, alphabetically, the names of these young members of the Keystone Little League team that was centered in the village of Beech Creek.

1. Landon Breon
2. Talon Falls
3. Alex Garbrick
4. Mike Keibler
5. Wyatt Koch
6. Tyler McCloskey
7. Brandon Miller
8. Trebor Nicodemus
9. Cole Reeder
10. Michael Smith
11. Ethan Watkins

Manager: Bill Garbrick   Coach: Justin Kline   Coach: Chip Miller

They and their mentors had a stellar season of Little League baseball. One after another, they won almost all their games. Their combined attitudes and abilities took them to the Little League World Series in South Williamsport, where they became the Little League champions of the entire eastern United States! Their record demonstrated that a wholesome team spirit helped a group of dedicated Clinton County athletes to run roughshod over excellent teams from throughout the country, until they were finally stopped by a team from the large California city of Huntington Beach; the city that then became the world champs. To the Beech Creek boys, we admiringly and respectfully dedicate this book. We thank them for taking us along on an incredible trip.

§ § §

IN GRATEFUL RECOGNITION

I offer special thanks to my wife, Nancy, who remains my first line of defense against literary sloppiness. Others who have contributed to making my work easier and more pleasant than I'd have guessed, must include Harold Adams, Harry Barner, Geneva Bauman, Tom Bauman, Lou Bernard, Thelma Bierly, Dotty Boyanowski, Ed Carothers, Loretta Coltrane, Margaret Coltrane, Edie Cox, Julie Klobe Divel, David Doerr, Charles Dorwart, Laura Eck, Tammy Farrington, Phil Feerrar, Wayne Feerrar, Sam Fuller, Margaret Garrett, Warren Gottshall, Todd Graybill, Fran Grugan, Richard Grugan, Gloria Harbach, John Harbach, Bob F. Johnson, Carol Kaler, Marge Kamus, Robert Kane, Amber Keene, Angela Koch, Travis Koch, Peggy Kurtz, Elizabeth Laurent, Douglas MacNeal, Bob Miller, Nell Muir, Troy Musser, Beulah Neff, Steve Neff, Russ Nelson, Michael O'Malley, Patricia Overdorf, Walter Overdorf, Ed Pickett, Dave Porter, Cecelia Ritter, Dave Ritter, Scott Sagar, Carol Segraves, James Segraves, Rod Segraves, Chris Shaffer, Rick Shaffer, Ed Snook, Gerrie Snook, Kirk Soverns, Marcella Soverns, Kathleen Tittle, Mary Lee Troup, Kim VanCampen, Wayne Welshans, Steve Weaver, Yvonne Weaver, Leroy Wenker, Terry Wenker, Bernard Wynn and the late Geraldine Bower Wynn.

No one left us with so large a variety of positive personal impressions of Prince Farrington as Tom Bauman of Castanea. Tom, who died on September 30, 2011, was appreciated while here and will remain a cherished memory

CONTENTS

Foreword

by
James Humes
Historian, biographer, Lycoming County native and speech-writer to five U.S. presidents.

I first met Guy Graybill in the Spring of 2001. He was doing the Lord's work – teaching history in a rural high school in a town with unpaved streets in southern Colorado blighted by poverty and despair. Most of his students were from families on welfare in this nearby one-time mining area which former presidential candidate, George McGovern, used as the subject of his doctoral thesis, writing on the violent strike in the early 1900's.

Guy Graybill is a gifted teacher with the innate talent of making history come alive by igniting his students' curiosity about events past and making them excited about study projects related to the assigned topic. Guy had invited me to share my experiences writing for five U. S. Presidents with his students. We were both teachers in Colorado far from our commonly shared roots in Central Pennsylvania. (I was then the Ryals Professor of Language and Leadership at the University of Southern Colorado – now Colorado State University at Pueblo.) We both shared a passion for Pennsylvania history and especially for the untapped lore of the Susquehanna Valley area. My first of 35 published books was "Sweet Dream – Tale of a River City," a history I was commissioned by the City of Williamsport to write for its centennial year. The title, "Sweet Dream," I took from a Coleridge poem, "May we ever follow the sweet dream/ Where Susquehanna pours its untamed stream." Coleridge, along with his fellow poets, Wordsworth

1

and Southey, was planning an artists' colony where the two Susquehanna branches – west and north- joined near Sunbury, close to Snyder County where Guy grew up. The Iroquois had their capital here where the rivers joined for their confederacy that spanned from Canada to North Carolina. My book, a chapter in which discussed their role in our Revolution, began with the Fair Play Men, near Jersey Shore, who met underneath an old elm tree called *The Tiadaghton* – the Indian name for Pine Creek – a tributary of the Susquehanna. When the tree fell in 1961, a gavel and salad bowl made from it were given to me. Settlers there on July 4, 1776, who were squatting on Indian territory beyond Philadelphia's jurisdiction, declared their own resolves for independence, completely unaware of what was taking place at the State House in Philadelphia.

Williamsport after the Civil War became for a time the world's lumber capital. Pine trees felled in northwest Pennsylvania were floated down the West Branch of the Susquehanna to lumber mills in Williamsport. Fortunes were made. The Williamsport High School team is still called the "Millionaires" because of the families made rich by the lumber trade.

I headed two historical societies, the Lycoming and Muncy, where I wrote articles on local history such as rafting or the building of the West Branch Canal. But one thing that never came up in our love for Central Pennsylvania history was Prince Farrington.

I knew the Prince's daughter, Gladys, and her handsome son, David Porter. In fact, David was once in my Sunday School class at the Jersey Shore Presbyterian Church. I was introduced to them by my aunt, Margaret Humes Collins, my late father's sister.

The house in Jersey Shore became our home in the early days of our marriage when we worked in Washington and Aunt Margaret became my surrogate mother with both of my own parents deceased. Because of her I wrote two books: "The House of Humes," on the Humes family and its pilgrimage from Scotland to Ireland to America, a thousand years. My aunt was fiercely proud of her Scotch Irish mountain roots. In her thirties, she moved to western North Carolina to build a school for illiterate mountain children. She had published two books of poetry celebrating her love of Scots mountain people, their culture and their ways, "Plenteous Heritage," and "Four Seasons." In the 1920's, she had traveled by rail across the country raising funds from D.A.R. chapters to fund schools to educate their illiterate kinsmen in the eastern mountains. Her favorite Jersey Shore Presbyterian Sunday School charge was David Porter, a darkly handsome and studious youth. His doting mother, the blowsy daughter of the Prince, would regale us with stories how they played Monopoly with real one hundred dollar bills. Gladys adored her oft-absent father, not unaware of his faults. The "Prince" was no Robin Hood, stealing from the revenuers and giving to the poor. But he could be generous to his family and to local churches. Until this book, I thought Prince was a name given to him for his princely purse (no, it was the name of the doctor who delivered him). My tee-totaling aunt, in a house that had never seen a drop of alcohol in its history spanning three generations, was enthralled by this prohibition Prince, but I remember her extracting a pledge from his grandson, David Porter: "Mrs. Collins, I swear to you I'm never going to touch a drop of liquor. I've seen too much of it in my family."

The Farringtons were Scotch-Irish. There was no Irish blood; they were Scots who emigrated to Northern Ireland and then to America in the middle of the 17th century. The Scots had evaded and defied English revenue agents and then U.S. ones in the early days of the Republic. The Whiskey Rebellion of 1796 was just one example of Scotch-Irish insurrection. The Scots gravitated to the mountains. The Appalachians from Pennsylvania to North Carolina, Kentucky and Tennessee became their home. They left the flat river land to the Germans who were the better farmers. "The Scots," said Aunt Margaret, "were better talkers – preachers, lawyers and politicians." She said that like Nixon, more Presidents were Scotch-Irish than anything else – Jackson, Polk, Buchanan, Hayes, Arthur and McKinley.

In 1960, I was a Fourth of July speaker underneath the 300 year-old Pine Creek Tiadaghton Elm. My subject was "The Fair Play Men" – that Scotch-Irish Presbyterian group who governed themselves separately from Philadelphia and wrote, as mentioned previously, their own Declaration of Independence. One of them had been my own forebear. A young listener, a student at Lycoming College, asked if it were difficult doing a talk when there were so few written records about the Fair Play Men. He was doing a college thesis on Prince Farrington and hoped to publish it as a book. I agreed to look over his material. I told him it was too sketchy and there was too little documentation for a book. On the contrary, Guy Graybill has written a researched, carefully footnoted account with recorded interviews; and what's more, it does not read like some dry college thesis. It is a lovely, fascinating account that brings a figure of local folklore to life. History, as Guy Graybill has proved in "Keystone," need not be a collection of dry statistics and dates. Just as he did in the classroom, he makes history a living thing and proves that local or regional history can reveal more about the culture, life and ethos of a people than a broader-scope national chronicle.

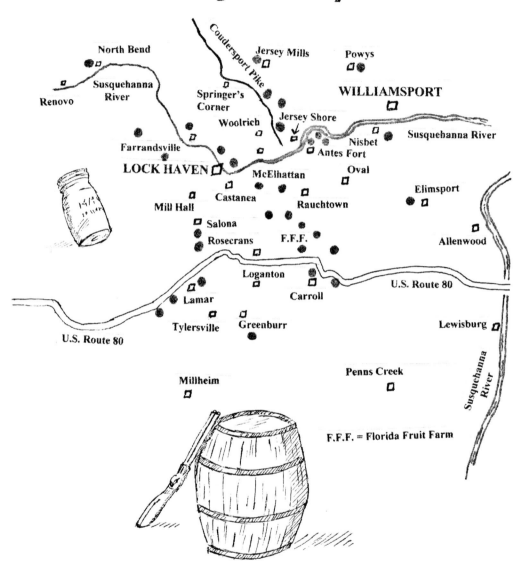

A Map of "Farrington Country" in Pennsylvania. The approximate locations of known still sites are represented by black dots. Additional sites are identified in Chapter Seven.

INTRODUCTION

Those of us who wrote and published *PROHIBITION'S PRINCE* were pleasantly surprised by the reception it received. It was not simply the robust local sales; but the many nice things that readers told us after they had read the book. Those kind comments, and the offers of much new information, made the preparation of this companion volume, *PRINCE AND THE PAUPERS*, a most pleasant experience.

One hates to spoil the mood; but we need to admit to several unintentional but real errors in the early copies of the first book. All imperfections that came to our attention have been corrected in recently printed copies. We learned of correct spellings for Segraves and Seyler, two names we had not seen in print; the improper use of the designations of *interstate* and *U.S.* for highways, and improperly crediting someone else for a statement by Jane Bubb Miller. The most disturbing error occurred when I was told that there were new operators for the *Gamble Farm Inn* of Jersey Shore. I wrongly assumed that this indicated new owners. In fact, that inn, once the home and business operation of Prince Farrington's daughter and son-in-law, has been under the ownership of Troy Musser for some years and it is Musser who is conducting historic changes to the property (see Chapter VIII). I offer sincere apologies to anyone who was affected by those mistakes. I'll do better.

Anyone who enjoys glancing into our past will enjoy three unique books about the area under discussion. These are the books from the Acadia Publishing Company's series, *Images of America*. These books combine superb period photographs and images with excellent captions. The three which we tout here are *Jersey Shore* and *Nippenose Valley*, both by Wayne Welshans and the one entitled *Sugar Valley Villages*, by David Ira Kagan and John W. Harbach, Sr. All are listed in the bibliography.

THE SPINNERS

The reference here, to 'spinners', is not to the political writers and pundits who offer 'spin' on events they wish to denigrate or to support. Here are the genuine spinners: the spinners of colorful recollections and rustic remembrances. These were, and are, the individuals who lived through the period under discussion and who recall or recalled incidents that, without their willingness to relate the past, would be beautiful images forever lost.

These departed spinners remarkably enriched the first volume of this biography: George Porter, Leo "Chip" Taylor, Thelma Matthews and Lester Seyler. Other spinners who added much to that first volume would include David Porter, Emily Farrington Packer, Miller Stamm, Harold "Dutch" Washburn, Tammy Farrington, and Charles Dorwart. Others, who gave smaller amounts of lore, are no less appreciated. All are listed with my expressions of gratitude.

Now consider what some of *this* volume's spinners have been able to add. Charles Dorwart, because of the variety of his experiences, has ~ once again ~ been a valuable resource. Tom Bauman, Prince's young neighbor, had years of interaction with Prince and his family. His remembrances were too unique to be matched by anyone else. Gloria and Jack Harbach also had direct contact with several of the important people discussed in this biography. James Segraves lived in the same house as one of Prince Farrington's close associates, James' dad, Colonel Segraves. Of the several good resources for the Klobes, Beulah Neff had the closest ties with Floyd Klobe and she possesses some of the finest relics and memories. Julie Klobe Divel and Thelma Bierly had much to tell about Herman and Charles Klobe. The sad saga of a town, *Alvira*, was spun with considerable scholarship by a pair of historians, Stephen C. Huddy and Paul C. Metzger (see the bibliography). We are especially grateful for the memories spun by the late Geraldine Bower Wynn, who was interviewed by her son, Bernard, just days before her passing, at the age of 88. Again, review the list of those to whom we all owe gratitude. The strength of this biography rests largely on the quality of our spinners.

NOTE: References to the first of these two books (*PROHIBITION'S PRINCE*) will appear throughout this book. They will be shown thusly, (I: 177), indicating, of course, that the reference is to *Prohibition's Prince*, at page 177.

§ § §

CHAPTER ONE

The Moonshiner, Revisited

THE NEEDED SUMMARY

Prince David Farrington (1889-1956), legendary, millionaire moonshiner /bootlegger, was born in Guilford County, North Carolina. Much about his childhood and early career is found in the first volume (*Prohibition's Prince*) of this two-part biography. After at least one local jail term and another term in the Federal Penitentiary in Atlanta, Georgia, Prince decided to take his wife, Martha ("Mattie") White Farrington (Marriage: October 4, 1912) and three children, Tom ("Huss"), Gladys Julia and Gayle Randall, to Pennsylvania. Keystone State geography seemed most favorable in Clinton and Lycoming counties. Recent figures show that Lycoming County is 75% wooded land, while Clinton County is more than 82% forested acreage. Both counties are overlaid with craggy landscape where small streams and thick forests provide two of the principal natural ingredients for moonshining: water and isolation. Prince Farrington bought a nicely developed fruit farm, *The Florida Fruit Farm*, in Greene Township, Clinton County, Pennsylvania. His farm was on the northern ridge that helped to form an agricultural enclave known as Sugar Valley. Eventually, a half-dozen cohorts in the moonshining business also came north.

Prince Farrington and his moonshining friends were in the Keystone State for only about a year before authorities made the first of several raids on one of his stills. Raids of this type would plague Farrington throughout most of his life. Prince's wife gave him a fourth child, Prince David Farrington, Jr. ("Whitey"), while they were living in Clinton County.

NOT EXCLUSIVELY A MOONSHINER

Prince Farrington, the nearly life-long moonshiner and bootlegger, had several forms of legitimate employment. Foremost among these would have been his farming. His farming lasted through much of his lifetime. However, during his early years in Pennsylvania he also made deliveries for a soft drink distributor and, during World War II, he worked in a defense job in the Allenwood-Alvira area.

Prince's involvement in his job at Allenwood was interesting for a couple of reasons. For one, Allenwood was the town from which Richard Baxter emerged. Baxter was the revenue agent who successfully pursued and apprehended Prince Farrington at his elaborate distilling operation on the Tangascootac Creek on August 27, 1946 (I:8-10). A second interesting fact about Prince Farrington's Allenwood-area employment: He had a legitimate form of employment during the 1940's in which he worked at a pump house, at Spring Garden, a settlement midway between Allenwood and Alvira. However, if local rumor is reliable, Farrington used that legitimate operation as a cover for operating another illegal still!

SOME VERY EMINENT DOMAIN!

In 1940, the village of Alvira sat about three miles northwest of Allenwood. The town consisted of a couple of dozen families, a pair of small stores, a blacksmith shop, and four churches. This charming village was surrounded by beautiful farms. The road that passed through the town was known as the Culbertson Trail and it was known to be a cross-country shortcut for shipments of Prince Farrington's whiskey that were being sent from Jersey Shore to Allenwood and to the thirsty markets beyond.

In early December of 1941 an act of war occurred nearly five thousand miles from Alvira. The Japanese warlords decided to attack a militarily-unready giant: the United States of America. Few towns or cities in America would feel the impact of that war more than the town of Alvira, Pennsylvania. No one in Alvira could have imagined that the distant war would obliterate their lovely little town in Union County, Pennsylvania. However, two town meetings – in February and March of 1942 – were held in the *Christ Lutheran Stone Church*. These meetings confirmed that the United States was going to buy about 8,000 acres in Alvira and the surrounding lands. The federal government was exercising the right of *eminent domain* and buying all the lands needed. The lands were to be purchased; but for prices that the landowners found to be pitiful. Even more stunning was the time frame. From the date of that second town meeting, all residents had to be gone from their Alvira homes within six weeks!

What had happened? The citizens of Alvira were quickly uprooted because the area, about 8,000 acres worth, was to be transformed into one of several sites to be used for creating mountains of TNT (trinitrotoluene) explosives for use against the three countries against which the United States Congress had declared war. The demands of war called for the quick destruction of the town, including the dynamiting and burning of buildings that had been businesses, schools, homes and two of the churches.

Within a few weeks, government agencies and private contractors were creating the buildings and concrete bunkers that were required for a major manufacturing complex. Many miles of roads and rails were built. Until huge trailer towns were established on the grounds, buses brought *defense workers* from Williamsport to their critical jobs in the Pennsylvania Ordnance Works. The explosives could now be made in gargantuan quantities and stored in the 150 new beehive-shaped bunkers. The Ordnance Works did not make bombs. The Pennsylvania Ordinance Works simply made the lethal ingredient that would be inserted elsewhere.

Alvira's corpse was never revived. Most of Pennsylvania's authentic ghost towns were the result of economic swings related to natural resources such as coal, lumber and oil. Alvira was unique. Instead of former landowners returning, different government entities carved the pilfered turkey. The U.S. Bureau of Prisons, in 1950, was given more than 4,000 acres, while the Pennsylvania Game Commission was granted more than 3,000 acres. The remaining acres went to numerous recipients of small tracts. Thus, instead of driving northwest from Allenwood and catching a sign saying "Village of Alvira," one reads a sign informing him or her that they have arrived at Pennsylvania's *State Game Land # 252*. The unfamiliar motorist cannot know the tragedy behind the sign.

Strangely, even this operation involved Prince Farrington. When a local resident saw a man (Huddy and Metzger, p. 32), hard-at-work, laying pipe into the Pennsylvania Ordinance Works, the man told the curious local that he was laying pipe and fixing the pump house. That seeming interloper was a hard-working Prince Farrington. Years later, former resident, Robert Russell, recalled (Huddy and Metzger, p. 33) "You know who ran the pump house down there at Spring Garden (a small settlement between Alvira and Allenwood)? Prince Farrington! They were having trouble with the pump there by the old iron bridge, and he got it going. What they didn't know was that he had a still set up in the pump house, too... made a nice fifth of whiskey, the man did... Well, when they finally closed him down and he went to trial at the courthouse up in Williamsport, guess what . . . all the evidence had 'run away'."

FARRINGTON'S METHODS OF OPERATION

Prince Farrington used a variety of skillful and innovative approaches to the hiding of his stills and their addictive distillate. Some failed and some were successful. Here are two such attempts.

Scientific advances are embraced with equal enthusiasm by the law-abiding and the lawless. Kerosene was processed, and so named, in Canada in 1854. It was found to be a non-volatile liquid that furnished light. Eventually kerosene also became a source of heat. At some point in his career, Prince Farrington began using kerosene to supply the heat needed for his distilling operations. Why kerosene? There was no tell-tale smoke to rise above the treetops. Science unwittingly supported moonshining.

Another Farrington method of deception was his loading of the perimeters of a truck-bed with crates of chickens, within which was a stash of whiskey. This specific mode was identified by Amber Keene, a native of Sugar Valley as well as the 93-year-old genealogist of the Rishel and related families. She now resides in historic Boalsburg (Centre County). Amber was also a descendant of the Poorman family that originally developed the lush orchards of the *Florida Fruit Farm*. Ms. Keene has related a specific, non-Farrington Sugar Valley incident worth recording. She tells of an aunt, Harriet (Hattie), who was married to Henry Karachner (the Karchners now omit the second '*a*' from their family name). One day, while Henry was away, their house caught fire. "Aunt Hattie" quickly laid the baby daughter, Helen, in a basket, picked up the basket, took her son, Clair, by the hand and escaped the burning house and ran across the field to a neighbor's house.

Even for Prince Farrington, the chance of being apprehended at a still was a real concern. Prince approached this dilemma by moving some stills; but he also used an increased number of stills and bribery as ways to increase his productivity. Prince might also have had others run stills for him. Even with Prince's several incentives, many individuals had their own stills. James Segraves has noted that phenomenon, with slight exaggeration: "Wherever there was running water, they made whiskey. They also kept moving the stills, to try to keep ahead of the revenuers."

PRINCE AND PRIME REALTY

For the past half century, Dora and Leroy Wenker have been regular patrons of the farm market in Lock Haven; but Leroy's story goes even further back in time. As a young farm boy, attending a tiny, rural school, Leroy shared one of the wide desks with young George Helvly. The Helvly's had a farm as well, just east of the Swissdale church; but their barn's hay mow (rhymes with 'cow') served a different function. Under the Helvly's hay mow there was also a stash of Prince Farrington's whiskey.

The young student, George Helvly, got diphtheria. Soon after, his desk mate contracted it too. The Helvly boy never recovered. He was buried in the Swissdale churchyard. But, Leroy Wenker's body was fighting. The doctor had asked Leroy's family if they had whiskey. He wanted Leroy to be given whiskey as a medication. They had none, so the Helvly's gave some whiskey to the Wenkers for young Leroy. With Helvly whiskey, the doctor's orders were followed. Leroy, given a tablespoon of whiskey each morning, survived the diphtheria.

The Wenkers lived along the Susquehanna, between Lock Haven and Farrandsville. They owned two farms on the south side of Bear Mountain, near Farrandsville. They also owned a tract of timber, containing almost 150 acres, on the north side of the mountain. One day, around the year 1940, Leroy Wenker was in the barn where he and his dad, Carl Wenker, were milking the dairy herd. Raymond Bauman, a friend of Carl and Prince Farrington, appeared at the barn door. He told Carl Wenker that Prince Farrington would like to talk to him. Leroy's dad told Raymond Bauman, "As soon as I get finished milking, we can go in the house and talk." Farrington and Bauman visited with Carl in the old farm kitchen. He had heard stories, both negative and positive, about Farrington. Young Leroy was impressed. Prince Farrington was visiting in *his* house. Leroy still recalls seeing Prince sitting in the old wicker rocking chair, and brushing his hand back over his balding pate as they talked.

Prince Farrington explained his interest. He wanted to buy the timber tract from Carl Wenker. Carl said that he had no interest in selling the land to Prince. Instead, he planned to sell the timber. Leroy observes, today, "Dad knew why Prince wanted to buy the land."

Another interesting picture of Prince came from his former personal driver, Sam Fuller. Sam says that Prince knew where every spring was located. While driving someplace, Prince instructed Sam to stop. They were at a roadside spring that Prince knew was there. Then Prince would have a swig of whiskey before turning up the brim of his hat. He'd put spring water into the brim and drink it as a chaser.

There was the constant threat of Prince or his helpers being caught. Despite the risk, people still went directly to the Stewart/Courtright farm to buy alcohol. Once, in 1933, Tom Bauman and his mother spent the night visiting different relatives in Lock Haven and close to Queen's Run, north of Lock Haven. When they telephoned for Raymond Bauman to come to get his wife and son, Raymond drove to the temporary bridge to cross the Susquehanna and enter Jersey Shore. The temporary bridge was actually the old bridge, which was being replaced. That temporary bridge was shifted slightly on railroad ties to one side. Then the new replacement bridge had been completed; but it had not yet been opened. Cars were allowed on the temporary bridge one-at-a-time. As Raymond waited for his turn to proceed, just one car was ahead of his. Bauman knew that the three occupants of the preceding car had been buying liquor from Prince. That car proceeded onto the bridge, which suddenly collapsed into the ice-swollen river. Raymond Bauman saw one of the men get out of the car and cling to some ice briefly; but all three drowned. Tom and his mother had to walk across the new and, as-yet, unopened bridge in order to rejoin Raymond Bauman for the sad trip home.

DOWN BY THE RIVERSIDE

At one point in time, Prince invited relatives to occupy his large farmhouse that was the centerpiece of the Gheen (today Courtright) property (I:151-156). These relatives were Prince's sister, Zenadah ("Nade") Coltrane, her husband, Kyle Coltrane and their three children, Hilda, B.W. and Wade. (I: many references). Tom Bauman, a neighbor boy in those days, recalls many visits to that farm. Memorable to the lad was the presence of large letters painted on the side of the tobacco shed. It was the name of one of the former owners: GHEEN. That name was visible from the highway, across the river. However, Bauman was more impressed with the matron of the house, although he never knew Zenadah Farrington Coltrane's real name. He says simply: "Nade was a beautiful woman." He explains: "I used to take my dog and we'd walk down between our farm and the Gheen farm. I can always remember this: Nade would see me coming and she would always have southern biscuits baked. *Always*. When I'd go in, she'd have one of them cut in half with butter and blackstrap molasses on, and a glass of milk.

"My mother later told me that Nade had cancer. She had an operation and they took her one breast; but it had already spread into the other one as well as into her bone structure. The cancer cut short the life of this fine lady. She was still living on the Gheen farm when she died; I think it was in the Williamsport Hospital. She was the first person I was around whose passing away really upset me."

PRINCE DAVID FARRINGTON was a child of the era. He had charm and generosity, with an untroubled knack for breaking laws. His reputation as a womanizer is also secure, as discussed in *Prohibition's Prince*. Ethel Klobe Quiggle often mentioned her impression: Prince liked women. He had an eye for women. Velma Williams (now Wolfe) was the sister of Prince Farrington's daughter-in-law, Martha (Mrs. Tom Farrington). Velma recalls having once been told, by Prince, that, "You're a fine looking young lady." Her friend, Tammy Farrington, observes that Velma, now in her tenth decade of life, and after bearing nine children, remains "an attractive lady."

MARTHA *WHITE* FARRINGTON ("MATTIE")

As mentioned earlier (I: 32), Martha ("Mattie") White Farrington (1895 – 1972), when visiting with Prince's sister in North Carolina, would sit for hours at a table and never offer to help with cooking or dishes. One might guess that this behavior was borne from her reluctance to associating with Prince's relatives. But, her own grandson, Robert, reinforces the image in his verse (I: 33), saying Mattie "Sat in the same chair most of the day, dusting only what she could reach..." Likewise, Tom Bauman, a young neighbor of the Farringtons when they were living on a farm near Jersey Shore, Pennsylvania, related, "The Farringtons never called me *Tom*. It was always *Tommy*. All except Whitey. All of them: Gladys, Tom and Gayle and Prince... even Matt (Martha). I remember her. She'd sit behind the kitchen table for hours and hours on end. Maybe she'd get up to go to the bathroom. When she came back, she'd sit right there again. I never saw her do anything so far as cooking was concerned. We'd come in from the fields and if we had a little ground on our shoes or anything, 'You hogdogs!' That was her favorite saying: 'You hogdogs!' She'd kind of give us all hell. Prince's favorite saying was 'Hell's bells!' if something went wrong. I can remember Prince saying that a good many times.

"Prince did all the cooking. He was a good cook. My favorite: For breakfast he made milk gravy on toast. And he always kind of burnt the flour before he put the milk in it, you know, and it was kind of brown. Geez, I could eat a good bit of that. Then he had a thing he would make, he would call it *succotash*; but my mother would call it *vegetable soup*. I remember, he used a pressure cooker and had that on the stove. He'd have a chunk of boiling beef in it. When it got done, you know, we'd get in there... and he'd get that piece of beef out and he'd slice it. He'd slice that down and then he'd put it on bread. He bought Italian bread all the time. He'd cover that with beef. While he was eating that, he had these hot Mexican peppers – about as big as your little finger – on a little dish and he would pick one up from there. I tried to eat one, one time. Oh! Oh! But, in all the time that I knew Prince, I never saw him eat a piece of pie... a piece of cake... or any candy. I never saw him eat any of those. He had no fascination for sweets."

A hint of Mattie's peculiar behavior was expressed by several individuals in *Prohibition's Prince* (I: 108-109, etc.). One day, recalled Ed Carothers, Prince and Mattie were going to a midsummer affair. Mattie came downstairs wearing a mink coat. Echoing remembrances that are similar was Tom Bauman, who mentioned an oddity of Mattie's, regarding clothing. "She always bought the best of everything. She would wear a dress for maybe three or four days; then she'd take it off, turn it inside-out, and wear it for another three or four days. She was eccentric like that, you know."

SIDE-BY-SIDE BURIAL PLOTS

There was considerable interaction between Prince, his wife and children and Prince's siblings and their families, as found throughout *Prohibition's Prince*.

There was some contact between Mattie's family and Prince's family, through Mattie White's sister, Hazel, who married Scott Anthony. They were parents of two children, Bernice and Lobby. Bernice married Howard Dodson, a very wealthy businessman from the Greensboro area of North Carolina. She died in 2011. Lobby's tragic fate is discussed in Chapter Four. Although many people interviewed described Martha White Farrington as being, at best, eccentric, her sister, Hazel White Anthony, was described as decidedly levelheaded and easy to be around. A legitimate question might be: Was Martha White naturally eccentric or 'odd', unlike her sister, Hazel, or did her choice of mates weigh more heavily on Martha than her fragile personality could bear? We must remind readers, again, that in 1929 Martha succeeded in obtaining a Lycoming County divorce from Prince Farrington; a divorce decree that never fully divorced them, since they still more-or-less remained as estranged partners right through their declining years and directly to their side-by-side grave plots at Burnett's Chapel in Guilford County, North Carolina.

PRINCE'S PROGENY

TOM "HUSS" FARRINGTON

Prince and Martha "Mattie" Farrington were parents to four children. There was no molding of offspring here. The four had vastly different personalities. Tom, who always carried the nickname, "Huss," within the family, was the oldest and, for a time it seemed, the wildest. "Unruly," was the word used to describe him in the earlier half of this biography (I:190). He got in trouble for intentionally scarring the Antes Fort school floor and, on a different occasion, for destroying some basement windows in that same Antes Fort school. He also did a lot of driving for his moonshiner father, including one unusual trip to Philadelphia. Tom drove his dad's Brockway truck. He may have been hauling booze to the city. He certainly was there to get a huge load of sugar. Tips regarding potential arrests were common, and when he got to the great port city, he was told that revenue agents were looking for him and his Brockway. Tom made a quick phone call to Prince for instructions. Prince's quick decision: "Trade the damned truck!" So Tom quickly got rid of his dad's Brockway and arrived home with a big load of sugar and a new Reo.

So, Tom Farrington's reputation wasn't expected to change with his pending marriage. After all, one is reminded: maturation and matrimony aren't always synonymous. Still, for Tom "Huss" Farrington, there seems to have been a substantial change. While his three siblings spent much of their lives struggling with employment and finances, Tom, once married, was transformed. He married a local contractor's daughter, Martha Williams. She sold cosmetics, with Tom sometimes acting as her driver. But, Tom also found steady employment at the Piper Aircraft Company factory in Lock Haven. His work with Piper likely kept him out of military service, since Piper was building large numbers of light aircraft that were useful to the military. Tom was the brother who, once an adult, never had trouble with the law. Tom, or "Huss" Farrington worked for the Piper Company until he retired, several years before the plant closed and some years before his death in 1986.

The Piper Aircraft Company was a fixture of Lock Haven industry for many years. Having begun in Rochester, New York, in 1927 as the *Taylor Brothers Aircraft Manufacturing Company*, they later moved – for a few short years – to Bradford, Pennsylvania. In 1937, the company moved to an abandoned silk mill in Lock Haven. That's where it became the *Piper Aircraft Corporation* and where it built its solid reputation. That facility was practically destroyed by the flood waters of Hurricane Agnes in 1972. Before the 1972 flood, the company had already begun moving its operation to Florida. The Lock Haven plant was totally closed in 1981. In recent decades the company has had a checkered history of ownership and production.

Meanwhile, the old Lock Haven plant has been converted once again. It is now the Piper Aviation Museum, with Russ Nelson as its principal researcher. It stands as a memorial to a company that once thrived by producing single engine, then twin engine, and, finally, jet engine planes for general aviation purposes. One early goal of the company was to create 'simple-to-pilot' aircraft. Thus, there is little wonder that nearly two-thirds of the Piper aircraft ever produced are still being flown!

GLADYS FARRINGTON PORTER AND HUSBAND, GEORGE

None who met her ever forgot her. Gladys Julia Farrington Porter was described as a 'character' whose speech was both plain and profane. She was the bootlegger's daughter who married her childhood sweetheart, George Porter, and bore him four children: Dave, Robert, Craig and Lisa.

From the standpoint of this biography, Gladys Julia is most significant as being a sometimes-effective and loyal supporter of her father, Prince. At one time or another, she and George managed a barroom in Mill Hall (for George's father); another at the mouth of the Tangascootac Creek, at another time, as well at the Broadway Hotel in Jersey Shore. Their memory, however, is best associated with the Gamble Farm Inn, in Jersey Shore. That inn has prospects for continued use and expansion, with the ownership of Troy Musser.

Tom Bauman's opinion of George Porter: "George was a likable guy; but he wasn't that energetic. I got a vehicle from him one time. George told me, 'Look, I'm gonna tell you something. Not all my vehicles are A-1; but I bought that one from a farmer and he used it to haul produce to markets. "It was a Dodge panel truck. I had it for about five years and it worked fine. It was kind of interesting to be around him." The author spent several hours in the company of Mr. Porter and he must concur with Bauman's opinion. George Porter was a very interesting individual.

Tom Bauman had been friends of all Prince's children. When Tom and Geneva Bauman visited Geneva's mother, in the Manor Care nursing facility in Lock Haven, Tom saw Gladys Porter in a wheelchair. She, too, had suffered some memory loss. Tom relates, "I walked over to her and I said, 'I bet you don't know who I am.' Gladys kind of sat back in the wheelchair… looked at me a little bit. Then she kind of got a grin on her face and she says, 'Tommy!' It wasn't too long after that that Gladys passed away. George hasn't been dead all that long. They're buried in the Jersey Shore cemetery."

GAYLE RANDALL FARRINGTON

His nephew, Dave Porter says that Gayle Farrington "was great to be around." Porter also remembers that Gayle gave him and his bride a very nice wedding gift. Although Dave also tells of his dad complaining that if it was easier to do something that was legal, Gayle would still do it the wrong way! Gayle is also fondly remembered by Tom Bauman. "Once they picked up Gayle down in Florida. He had scammed a couple of guys who had a shoe-repair business. They were sleazy bastards!"

And now, whether or not the shoe repair owners were sleazy, Gayle had swindled them out of some money. So there was a warrant for his arrest. When Gayle was found in Florida, he was returned to Clinton County.

Thanks to Tom Bauman's description, readers can sense the atmosphere in a relaxed, rural county jail. As Bauman recounts the scene: "They had always been my lifelong friends, you might say. I knew Sheriff George Hickoff, so I told my wife, 'I'm going to go over and see if I can see Gayle. So I went over. Hickoff could have been sheriff until he was a hundred and five years old. He was a heck of a nice guy. It got so that they couldn't even get someone to run against him for sheriff. Anyhow, I went over and went into the office. The sheriff was talking with someone. He asked, 'Can I help you?' and I said, 'I just wondered if I could see Gayle Farrington. I hear he's in here.' 'Yeah', Hickoff said, 'He's back there. Go on back'. I went back. The cell door was open. Robert Farrington (Charl Farrington's oldest son) and Huss (Prince Farrington's oldest son) were already in there visiting. All three were sitting on the jail cot, talking.

"I walked in and we shook hands all around. I hadn't seen Robert for quite a while. Robert was married to a good friend of my wife and I used to see him pretty often. Gayle was always likable. We sat there talking. I asked them where their dad was. I wasn't absolutely sure that the authorities had picked him up; but they had got him soon after they got Gayle.

"Then these two brothers who had the shoe business came in. They had recently talked to Tom ("Huss") on the telephone. One of them said to Huss, 'Well, I see they picked up the old man. It's too bad the old bastard didn't die,' or something like that. Well! You didn't say something like that to Huss! They had said this on the phone. Boy, when they walked in the cell, Huss was up off that cot and I thought he was going to clobber those guys! If it hadn't been for Robert and Gayle grabbing him, he would have clobbered them. And he was capable of cleaning them up. He was a pretty wiry guy. I thought, 'What the hell is going on?' but Gayle said, 'Let me talk to them.' Gayle (the brother that they said had swindled them) stepped out into the hall with those two. I don't know what he said. Anyway the two brothers left.

"It wasn't too long after that that those two brothers (who operated the shoe business) were put in jail. They were making girlie movies in their store and one of the girls turned them in to the police and the police raided them. They had all these movies that they had made – and there were three or four girls involved – and so they ended up in jail.

"That was the last time that I saw Gayle; but, as I said, I worked at Piper with Huss.

17

"Gayle had moved out and was living near Dayton, Ohio. He was still a little shaky in business. One day (at Piper) a co-worker (name omitted) came over to me. He said 'We were just out and visited Gayle. He's up to his old tricks. He's selling real estate.' One day this same person came in and he saw me. I was on test flight (a job Bauman did at Piper aircraft company for several years) and I was going up to the office for some reason. I passed the department he was in. 'Hey! Hey Tom!' He says, 'Your friend, Gayle, sold non-existent real estate and now he's in jail.'" Gayle had to face charges a number of times, in both state and federal cases. While spending some time in jail, Gayle was viciously attacked, with his skull being visibly damaged. Gayle Randall Farrington died several years later of a brain tumor.

PRINCE DAVID "WHITEY" FARRINGTON, JR.

The youngest child of Prince and Mattie was rarely addressed as 'Prince'. He went through life simply as 'Whitey,' from his school days until he died. He was remembered (I: 61) for the time he innocently washed some of his dad's illicit paper money because he heard his mother complain about the 'dirty money' that his father obtained. He was also remembered (I: 60), by his poorer Southern cousins for having an actual mechanical toy automobile, a rare toy reserved only for the wealthiest youngsters of the time. More recently, a former neighbor recalled hearing young Whitey saying, "Daddy, I need some change."

"Whitey was a wild one," observed Sam Fuller. Gigging fish or frogs involves spearing them with a long, metal rod with illegally attached fishhooks. Gigging was done from a rowboat or canoe and it was done at night with a flashlight, when the frogs weren't so easily disturbed. Gigging was, and remains, illegal. Fuller accompanied Whitey on gigging trips. Fuller held the flashlight, while Whitey gigged frogs, to obtain their hind legs for cooking and eating. Sam Fuller also tells of a group of teens going 'out on the town' with Whitey, in his 1941 *Lincoln Zephyr.* "He was crazy. He'd get half whacked. Prince gave him hell for speeding!"

Whitey speeding? Tom Bauman has similar memories.

While living in State College, Prince David Farrington, Jr. ran off with someone else's wife, fathered a child with her and, apparently still unmarried, left her to go to Florida. Years later, now in his sixties, he sister, Gladys, reportedly struck him with her purse and her sailor's tongue, calling him a "son of a bitch!" for considering marriage to a woman in her twenties. Yet, his nephew, Dave, remembers that Whitey had given him a $100.00 wedding gift; a substantial sum in that place and time.

Prince David Farrington, Jr., the man who carried the moonshiner's name, also spent time in jail for the cabin-rifling incident mentioned above and in the first volume (I: 191). He may have emerged as Prince's unruliest son, if one judges by his very fast driving, his adventures with women and his occasional brushes with the law.

Bauman is blunt: "Whitey always drove like hell! He was a good driver; but he always drove fast." Bauman then goes on to tell of a time that he and his wife were visiting his mother on the farm to which they had moved, near Lock Haven. At the time, Whitey's brother, Gayle, had a used car lot on Bellefonte Avenue in Lock Haven. The night that Tom and Geneva were visiting his mother, Whitey was apparently speeding again. He was driving up Church Street with cops chasing him. He led them on a high speed chase. He knew he could turn on Park Street and zip down to the river, cross the railroad and race down around the creek road and over to the home of Tom Bauman's mother. There was one small catch....

Whitey turned on the wrong street. He was racing toward the canal that provided water for the paper mill. Knowing that the police would soon be coming down that same street, he couldn't turn around. He must either stop or drive into the canal. So he slammed the brakes, stopped his car and jumped out. Since he had a small head start, he ran, unseen, along the canal and across the railroad. Then he plunged into Bauman's cornfield!

Tom Bauman, his wife, and his mother, were sitting and chatting in his mother's living room. His mother said, "Somebody's in the kitchen." Tom went to investigate. There was Prince David Farrington, Jr., 'Whitey' to all the Baumans who were present. He was soaking wet from the neck down, from running through the cornfield.

Bauman asked, "What'n the Hell happened?" Whitey's response: "Oh, Jesus! Can you take me over to the *Sons of Italy*?" Bauman repeated, "What in the Hell happened?"

Then Whitey explained the chase. His solution, which Tom helped him to achieve:

Tom drove the Bauman's old V-tag truck that they used on the farm and for hauling coal on occasion. He took Whitey to the Lock Haven lodge of the *Sons of Italy*. Whitey went into the lodge and found his brother, Gayle, the auto dealer. Gayle, businessman that he was, joined various social clubs. Whitey told Gayle about the chase and all. Then he asked Gayle to: "Call the police like you are leaving, and tell them that your damned car has been stolen!" Gayle certainly didn't want anyone to know that Whitey was in the *Sons of Italy* with him and that

Whitey had taken that car. The ruse worked. No one ever found out. The paper reported that a car was stolen from Gayle's parking lot.

Then, there were the trips that Tom Bauman and Whitey Farrington took to Altoona. Prince had been raising sweet corn on the farm of Wesley Koch. Prince had recently bought a new Ford pickup truck. Tom Bauman and Whitey were given the job of filling the new truck with sweet corn and hauling it to Altoona to sell, door-to-door. They loaded about 200 dozen ears onto their truck and drove it to Lock Haven to Johnny Ripley's ice plant. There they scattered several kegs of ice onto the corn to keep it fresh before setting off, in the wee hours, for Altoona. Once in Altoona, they'd have breakfast then drive into a neighborhood and make just one stop. Word quickly spread through the streets, neighborhood to neighborhood. Within about four hours, their couple thousand ears of corn were sold and they could return home.

Sam Fuller wasn't the only one impressed by Whitey's lead foot. It was while leaving Altoona on one visit that Bauman saw his best evidence of Whitey's passion for speed. He came to a rise in the road. Bauman glanced at the speedometer. The needle was at 100! Whitey had to quickly slow because of the road conditions, which put his speed down to where the state policeman they passed didn't even stir.

Despite Whitey's somewhat more advanced age, he and Tom Bauman worked and socialized together. Even after the Baumans moved to the Castanea area, outside Lock Haven, Tom, who was just entering his teens, would break down a shotgun, wrap it in a burlap bag and peddle his bicycle all the way to Prince's home outside Jersey Shore. Then Bauman and Whitey would go hunting together.

Still, Whitey worked as hard as he played. He is often seen working on the farm. In support of a smoother operation, Whitey taught young Bauman how to drive a 1938 Ford one-half ton pick-up truck. He also sold his dad's sweet corn to the produce-starved people of Altoona. He also ran a trap line as a young man. Briefly, Whitey was also in the used-car business and, at one period of his life, he worked for the Tennessee Valley Authority. And, Whitey was the only one of Prince Farrington's sons who was in the military service. He got his basic training in Texas, before going to Nebraska for schooling as a gunner on a 4-engine, propeller-driven B29 Superfortress bomber. He was still in training when the war ended, so Whitey never left the States.

Tom Bauman's memories of his last two encounters with a lifelong friend: "The last couple of times I saw Whitey... he had that used car lot up on Hogan Boulevard (outside Lock Haven). He introduced a woman to me as his wife. And she had two kids. I don't think that they were Whitey's. They were too old. Then I didn't see him again until I was up at the *Pine Creek Inn* one night. I was going in there and he was coming out. He was by himself. I guess he was in there having a few drinks. I saw him there and talked with him for a few minutes before he got into the car and left. That was the last time I saw Whitey."

There is a story out of Lycoming County that harks back to the waning days of Prince Farrington's career. It has been said that Prince Farrington gave one of his last stills to his sons. However, the boys neglected to dismantle and hide the still before hunting season. Hunters saw and reported the still. Revenue agents then went to the still and blew it up.

THE GRAND HOLIDAY OF DECEMBER 5, 1933

Prince David Farrington was determined to be a moonshining outlaw. While the 18th Amendment (1919) outlawed the manufacture, transporting or sale of alcohol, Farrington had already been making untaxed and illegal liquor before the amendment was passed. During the ensuing 14 or so years, while *Prohibition* was in effect, Farrington was defying the 18th Amendment and its supporting laws by moonshining. Finally, when the 21st Amendment replaced the 18th Amendment, Farrington briefly tried the legitimate route; but soon returned to the secluded stills of the moonshiner.

Those addicted to alcohol and those who simply loved to consume it, were 'chompin'- at-the-bit' for the end of Prohibition. From the sots to the social drinkers, the return to legalized alcohol could not come fast enough. Obviously, imbibers spirits (pardon the pun) were lifted when, in 1932, Franklin Delano Roosevelt promised that if he was elected to replace President Herbert Hoover, he would push for repeal of the much-trampled 18th Amendment. When Congress, in early 1933, issued the text of the proposed 21st Amendment, it allowed a seven-year period for the required two thirds of the states to accept it. Seven long years? They needed less than ten months!

The way many people celebrated, December 5, 1933, one would have thought that the nation had just won its independence, or that the First World War had just ended. Instead, great hosts of the American public were celebrating the passage of the 21st Amendment to the U.S. Constitution. One by one the states had voted to ratify the proposed new law. On December 5, 1933, at 5:32 P.M., Utah approved ratification. The requisite number of ratifying states had been reached. Less than two hours later, President Franklin D. Roosevelt issued the proclamation damning the 18th Amendment to perdition. The grand celebration that followed was in observance of the end of legally-enforced temperance. The 21st Amendment, passed on December 5, 1933 was ratified, presumably, to end the lawlessness and mayhem of the 1920s. It was during that era of anti-Prohibition lawlessness, that Al Capone, Dion O'Banion, Benjamin "Bugsy" Siegel, Joseph Kennedy, Prince Farrington and many others, made their fabled fortunes. Still, that lawlessness was replaced by the mayhem of drunken driving that takes thousands of American lives annually. However, the temperance advocates were properly chastened; never to raise their lemonade-drenched voices again. The proclamation of December 5, 1933 acknowledged the triumph of the lawless minority. They had regained their booze! All was right with the world.

The end of Prohibition posed a real dilemma for Prince David Farrington. People could now legally buy their spirituous liquors. They could also pay normal market prices. Still, after Prince tried, unsuccessfully, to do some legal distilling or brewing, he fell back on his skills and on his reputation for making superior quality whiskey. He re-entered the misty haunts of the moonshiner.

CHAPTER TWO

The Politicians' Poverty

POVERTY ~ 2008 VERSION

During the national elections in 2008, candidates from both major parties sought more voter support by promising to address the terrible economic conditions that squeezed the nation's citizenry. While some individual citizens were without jobs and some surely felt an economic pinch, the economic issue was an example of *politician's poverty*; a phony issue foisted on a gullible electorate.

NOTE: If the reader has trouble recognizing sarcasm, kindly skip the following few paragraphs and move to the next major topic.

Was Hunger really stalking the land? Were masses of Americans really facing wintry blasts without warmth? Were the nation's children really barefoot and leaving bloody footprints in the snow? Or did the Great Depression of 2008 actually qualify for a more precise label: Bullscat?

2008 was the year that saw Americans in their threadbare jackets standing in queues in order to spend (weekly!) more than *a hundred million* dollars to gain entrance to theaters, plus additional *millions*, weekly, for the opportunity to rent or buy DVDs that peddled motion pictures where "Vulgarity, " and "Violence" are frequently the primary stars.

2008 was the year that saw Americans, not knowing from whence their next meal was coming, spending countless *billions* of dollars in order to enter the great chain of food kitchens known as *Fast Food*, while turning gluttonous contest winners into celebrities! The nation's impoverished economy supports enough overeating to turn America into a giant flab lab.

2008 was the year that saw barefooted Americans paying hundreds of dollars per family outing in order to see athletes, who struggled to get by on a $15 to 20 million-dollars-per-year salary performing between the taping of endorsement ads that gave them additional millions of dollars!

2008 was also the year that saw Americans sneaking away from the bread lines in order to spend long hours in lines that allowed them to spend *billions* of dollars on the latest technological gadgetry and junk, much of it expressly created for the child and the child-like in America.

2008 was one more year that saw America's penniless populace investing more than 50 *billion* dollars on the purchase of illegal drugs!

2008 was the year that saw America's destitute crowds spending *billions* of dollars in order to play the rigged games that are known as state lotteries or feeding the rigged machines of the nation's glitzy slots parlors. Further, members of our famished nation were able to lose *billions* of dollars to a single Ponzi scheme!

In 2008, once again, we saw poverty-pleading Americans spending many *billions* of scarce dollars on America's royal class: our children. This youthful royalty, with no visible source of income, supports an aging teen queen and dips into a bottomless royal purse that allows them to spend, for example, hundreds of millions of dollars on a single line of dolls, all of which look alike if one looks closely at the eyes and the anorexic limbs.

2008 was the year that saw America's great hordes of hoboes spending *billions* of dollars on alcoholic drinks in order to participate in the great national binge.

Of the billions upon billions of dollars spent, in one year, on the above purchases, which ones were vital to the physical, or even the *emotional* health, of our spendthrift population?

What a paradox! The government established guidelines for identifying the victims of poverty, so that sociologists could gather data on the immense buying power of the poor!

This modern, political poverty, finds Americans shopping, not to acquire; but simply *shopping to shop*! Then, once having accumulated more purchased goods than they can accommodate, they rent storage sheds, cram attics to the rafters and hold endless yard sales.

Poverty, indeed!

WHEN *REAL POVERTY* STALKED THE LAND

Two Biblical spokesmen for Jesus, his apostles Matthew (Chapter 12) and Luke (Chapter 21), tell of Jesus observing a widow putting two of the land's tiniest coins into the temple collection. As Jesus explained, the widow's contribution was far greater than the larger sums given by the wealthy, since it was virtually all that she had. *That* was poverty.

Charles Dorwart, as mentioned before (I: 193) recalled his mother feigning a lack of hunger when there was insufficient food available for the evening meal. Dorwart could readily identify with the Biblical accounts of the widow's mites, since he remembers his mother giving each of her children a penny to put into the collection plate in Sunday School. Living within the poverty that was aggravated by a father who had an unabated "lust for booze," young Charles Dorwart worked on farms, for a small pay and a meal; but sometimes the strenuous farm work provided only the meal. While the town of Antes Fort, where Charles lived, had few substantive jobs, he earned small amounts of income from the farm jobs, plus lawn mowing and, as a teen, from staying overnight with elderly individuals. In that last line of employment, Dorwart several times had to run to one of the only two households in Antes Fort that had telephones, in order to place emergency calls. The accumulation of an extra dollar became the entertainment portion of his income. This was used for a movie at Jersey Shore's *Victoria Theater*, for 15 cents, plus a hot dog and a milk shake. Charles Dorwart, who later organized the Antes Fort museum in the old school building, has a vivid memory of the time that the ticket seller told him that he appeared tall enough and old enough to pay the 25-cent adult ticket price. One other aspect of the economic life of young Charles Dorwart matched that of the poorest folks across America: Charles helped his mother to take in the washing and ironing of other families, with the washing being done in a tub on their back porch.

HAND ME DOWNS AND NATURE'S HARVEST

Geraldine (Bower) Wynn was born (1923) in the Rosecrans area of Sugar Valley and lived there, on Rockey Road (I: 90-94) until required to move into the extended care facility in Lock Haven Hospital for the last three years of her life. Mrs. Wynn told her interviewer, her family consisted of her parents, two siblings and herself. Although poor, she said that they always had enough to eat and to wear, as well as a warm place to sleep. Her dad, Harry Bower, worked in the early lumber industry, cutting timber. Her mother, Maggie (Duck) Bower, helped tend their cow and chickens. An occasional pig, purchased from a neighbor, would be butchered for the additional meat. A neighbor would bring his horse and plow to prepare their land for planting. When Harry borrowed a team of mules, on one occasion, young Geraldine got experience in harrowing the fields. Here, again, the age-old practice of gathering brought the family extra food, from their haul of huckleberries, chestnuts and 'honeysuckle apples' (the small, light green and tart fruit of the wild honeysuckle bush). Her dad also supplemented the family's diet by hunting and fishing. Bear meat was also on their menu, and Geraldine remembered a lady guest asking for an onion that she could eat, in order to modify the taste of her bruin feast.

Mrs. Wynn also observed that those neighbors who didn't own tillable land suffered much more from poverty than those who had truck patches or gardens. Geraldine's berry picking helped to finance her clothes. Hucksters, buying and selling to rural folk, visited locally. There was also the 'ragman' who would gather old clothes, papers and other unwanted items. Fortunately for Geraldine, the ragman stored some things in her grandfather's shed. This arrangement allowed the inquisitive girl to look at his stock. It was there that she found some hymnals that she was able to give to an impoverished, nearby church group that was meeting in a tent. The storage shed was where she also spied an attractive dress which she asked for and which she was given. From their own accumulated rags, the Bower family quilted bedding and braided rugs.

Geraldine Wynn said that they walked wherever they went, including the one-room elementary school where she and her siblings studied. That was a one-mile jaunt. Her teacher also took the students to one of the larger farms, to teach them how to square dance. Then, as now, Memorial Day was the occasion for a parade and ball game in Loganton. An even-more-special day was when a circus came to Loganton. Geraldine and her mother walked the two miles to that event, although the youngster had trouble staying awake for the long walk home.

The creation of the Civilian Conservation Corps as a federal work program put young men to work in many areas far from home. Many of the CCC projects involved building woodland roads. CCC workers were paid $25.00 per month, with $20.00 being sent home and the worker was allowed to have the $5.00 to squander as he wished during the upcoming month. How many romances were kindled by the presence of Civilian Conservation Corps camps in an area? How many young CCC workers were enchanted by attractive local girls or, conversely, how many local females' heart fluttered at the sight of the neatly-uniformed stranger to their area? Apparently, a solid marriage resulted from the meeting (I:

63) of the local girl, Thelma Witmyer, and the CCC member from Texas, Milburn Matthews. Here, too, another Sugar Valley romance: Geraldine Bower and a CCC worker from the Rauchtown area, named Arthur Wynn.

Although it was thought that her dad's family had some dealings with the valley's noted moonshiner, Prince Farrington, Geraldine Bower Wynn's maternal side of the family had little or nothing to do with Farrington. Geraldine did recall, however, that her mother never said anything critical of Prince Farrington. To her mother, Farrington was a benevolent man who helped people who were in need.

Although Geraldine Bower Wynn died in the hospital in Lock Haven in early 2011, her body was returned for burial to the Mount Pleasant Cemetery at Rosecrans, about three miles from the home where she had been born.

WHEN THE LESS TYPICAL WAS TYPICAL

Like Charles Dorwart, and the late Geraldine Bower Wynn, many of the older citizens of Lycoming and Clinton counties in Pennsylvania remember living through, or hearing parents graphically describe what *real poverty* was like. Real poverty involved extending the lives of badly worn leather shoes by putting strips of rubber automobile inner tubes or pads of newspaper pages inside. Similarly, the Depression-era generation remembers clothing being handed down, altered to fit, and then being handed down once again. Clothing, that became too worn to wear, was cut into pieces to become the makings of patch quilts or coverlets. Feed mills became the boutiques where poor folk bought used and patterned cloth feed bags to be used for clothing, curtains, etc. Plain feed bags, on the other hand, were sewn into bedding and kitchen towels. Bed sheets - once they became too worn through the middle - were cut and re-sown, with the edges now seamed to form the middle. Cloth that, seemingly, had reached the end of the line, simply assumed a new utilitarian form: the dust cloth. Today, the only folks wearing threadbare clothing are the millionaire country singers!

It may be difficult for most citizens of our gluttonous nation to remember shortages of food or the lack of choices even when food was available. When beef, pork or poultry was served at the dinner table, the bones may already have been extracted in order to boil for a weak broth. If there was no meat available, a poor-person's gravy was made by browning flour in a pan of simmering water. Some families used the dried root of the common chicory plant to create a substitute coffee. Coffee grounds, where used, were often saved to be dried and used another time, while eggshells and vegetable parings were scattered in the family garden to enrich the soil. School lunches were often sparse; with the poorest youngsters carrying only an unbuttered sandwich, spread with lard. The more fortunate students carried sandwiches spread with home-made fruit preserves. There might also be seasonal fruit or a hard-boiled egg. Farm youngsters might enjoy a lunch that included water cress sandwiches. Many rural family members helped fill the family dinner plate by gardening, hunting wild game, fishing the creeks, gathering the seasonal harvest of wild nuts and berries or by hunting wild game. Richard Grugan has observed that, "They didn't hunt for fun as much then. They hunted for food." Another example of successful scavenging for food: dandelion, a despicable weed today, was a welcome dish, served with a savory bacon dressing, on many Depression-era dinner tables.

For rural folk, the preserving of food was a natural activity. Bernard Wynn, grandson of a Sugar Valley farmer who also did both driving and hiding of Prince Farrington's moonshine, mentioned an activity rarely seen today: the smoking of meats. The wood to be burned for the smoking process would be dead chestnut, mixed with either sassafras or maple or hickory. Other types of wood might smoke or 'cure' the meats; but they wouldn't enhance the flavor. Add to the home-style preservation of foods, the order in which foods had to be consumed, with perishables eaten quickly and the other foods smoked or, with produce, stored in underground bunkers or within cellars. From the proper preservation and storage came the feasts of fall and winter. On the other hand, Marie Segraves was remembered for the canning of venison.

A FUEL WORTH STEALING FOR

When the train stopped at Antes Fort, it was common for local citizens to wait for a compassionate engineer to toss down a few chunks of coal, in order for those below to gather the welcomed fuel for their homes. One can imagine this happening many times, in many towns, across the country. In fact, Harry Barner told of something similar occurring in nearby Jersey Shore. There, we're told, there was a slight grade in the railroad tracks. So someone would grease those tracks. While the engineer struggled to get his train off the greased slope, locals would climb onto the more isolated coal-laden cars and unload some of the precious chunks of carbon fuel.

One childhood incident related by Bob F. Johnson of the McElhattan area: As a youngster, he and his father, George Johnson, cut a lot of lumber with a crosscut saw. His father also farmed for others. Robert, as a boy, climbed onto a car of an idle coal train and tossed a small pile of coal to the ground. After the somewhat lighter train chugged from the area, he went home and told his father what he had done. The father first scolded him for the theft and then hitched his horse to a wagon and went to gather the booty.

Bob Miller's memories were interesting for his remembrances of little improvements that came into his family's life. He remembered the addition of electricity to his life, in 1942 and the purchase of a used Farmall 8 tractor, with its stud wheels.

GLEANING

The public recognition of 'charity' has roots as old as the Old Testament of the Christian Bible. There is the specific admonition (Leviticus: 19:9-10), "And when ye reap the harvest of your land, thou shalt not wholly reap the corners of thy field, neither shalt thou gather the gleanings of thy harvest. And thou shalt not glean thy vineyard, neither shalt thou gather *every* grape of thy vineyard; thou shalt leave them for the poor and stranger. I am the LORD your God."

Further, one of the great pastoral tales in the Bible, as well as its most romantic story, is the one found in the second chapter of the book of Ruth. Here the reader is treated to a love story, the story of a celebrated marriage between a Hebrew and a Moabitess, and the story of fulfilling one's obligation to the poor. The gleaning field was the setting for the meeting of Boaz, the land owner, and Ruth, the widow and barley gleaner who was to become his wife.

Rural Americans, during the era of the Great Depression, experienced the phenomenon of gleaning. John Muthler adds a local view to the picture of gleaning. John was a young man when Prince Farrington lived on the adjoining farm between Antes Fort and Jersey Shore. Muthler recalls having relatives who lived in Cogan Valley, off Route 287, in the area of White Pine and Brookside. Those relatives raised peas for a cannery. This was just one of many places where one could see the Biblical tradition of gleaning still being observed. Local people, Muther remembers, were allowed to come into those Cogan Valley fields to gather peas that the machines hadn't harvested.

PRINCE: A WELCOME PRESENCE

If a new plant moved into an area, everyone recognized its economic potential immediately. When the new moonshiner moved into Clinton and Lycoming counties in Pennsylvania, the realization was slower to happen. The economic impact of this entrepreneurial moonshiner was assured; but not obvious. The acceptance of Prince Farrington and his fellow outlaws came about slowly, helped by his liquid assets and his cash on hand. A stranger who wanted to give money to people who would help him cook and carry his liquor wouldn't remain a stranger for long. An equally enthusiastic welcome came from those people who craved the alcoholic drinks that were, from 1919 until 1933, illegal to make, market and consume. Many local people were eager to bend and break stifling laws in order to help Prince by working for him and/or by buying his superior quality whiskey for their own superior quality thirsts.

A hint of Prince's economic impact would be found in the comments of Dave Ritter's dad. Dave noted that his dad had a saying, "It didn't take too much to know who was running moonshine for Prince, because they usually drove a fairly new car." This couldn't be better illustrated than by viewing the photo of the three members of the Meixell family who worked with Prince Farrington. All had new cars!

One image of Prince is as an employer of children. He hired people to work for him. Older teens might be given an advance in order for them to be able to buy a bicycle. This would give them transportation to his farm. He was also known for hiring younger, local Antes Fort-area children. They were usually less than ten years old. He'd pay about eight cents an hour. Then he led the toddlers to the field to hoe corn. They were also admonished to *stay out of the rye*! They were then left to labor, unsupervised. He'd return to find them playing "hide and seek" in the rye. Prince would chastise them and fire them! But, the next day Farrington would be back, hiring the same urchins in an on-going effort to get a good corn crop. While his methods may seem harsh, he still paid slightly more than other employers of young folk.

AN ISOLATED FARM TALE

Charles Dorwart, whose memory has repeatedly given readers glimpses of early 20th century life of the Antes Fort/Jersey Shore areas of Lycoming County, also recalled another personal incident. As a youngster, he worked on the tenant farm of the Fox family. That farm was located just east of Antes Fort. While Dorwart was working on the wagon behind the baling machine, he swung the large hook used to capture the emerging hay bale and pull it onto the wagon. At that instant, the baler lurched, and young Dorwart got a severe gash in his ankle. Also revealing the special strength of childhood ties: Dowart notes that today there are no members of the Fox family living in Antes Fort, yet several family members still drive the extra miles in order to return to the town's United Methodist Church for Sunday worship.

A MODERN SPINDLETOP?

During the latter half of the1800s, Pennsylvania was the premier oil producing state. However, the Keystone State was replaced as the nation's great oil center with the discovery of the rich quantities of petroleum that lay beneath the surface of Texas and Oklahoma. Near Beaumont, Texas, on January 10, 1901, the discovery of an incredible bed of oil ushered in the modern age of oil drilling and retrieval. The site was known as *Spindletop.* It was after the discovery at Spindletop that oil finally moved past coal as a national fuel source. The abundance of oil also helped produce the nation's proliferation of automobiles and trains.

A SIMILAR STORY, REPEATED

Prince David Farrington's moonshining and bootlegging had little impact on the environment. Purists would have trouble even locating his work sites; much less seeing any environmental harm resulting therefrom. However...

As the early 21st century unfolded, many were, once again, lamenting hard economic times. While the economy of the Clinton/Lycoming counties' area was far richer than it was during Prince Farrington's heyday, employment had become harder to find and harder to keep. Once again, a new source of wealth appeared. This new 'moonshine' was also produced in the hinterlands, such as the forests north of Lock Haven and Swissdale. Trucks could be seen, at almost any hour, driving into and out of the mountains. New money was arriving in what was once "Farrington Country." The name of the new commodity was not "white lightening," however, and it was not hidden in false fenders and gas tanks. This was natural gas and it was turning the area into "Marcellus Country." This fuel comes from a gas-rich geological phenomenon known as Marcellus Shale. The gas is found in a stratum that lies about 8,000 feet beneath our own feet. A mixture of water and chemicals is pumped into the earth, in a process identified as 'fracking' so that the gas is primed for removal or for capping for future extraction. Today, Pennsylvania is one of a quartet of states that sit astride this trillion-dollar treasure.

The number of new wells involved in this boom is expected to eventually shoot past the 100,000 figure! Williamsport, some are predicting, will become the state's third great economic hub, forming a triangle with Pittsburgh and Philadelphia. The companies that are among the energy giants of America are now drilling into the region's rich beds of Marcellus shale gas. The purchase of mineral rights and the tapping into the local economy, are creating wealth for distant entrepreneurs as well as for local landowners, business owners and field workers. As happens with many technological advances, there is the mix of culture shock and bulging wallets. In a single day, one can observe the many noisy, road-mangling trucks hauling water from the Susquehanna to the new drilling sites; while also noticing the men in hard hats who are carrying boxes of meals from the local eateries. A modern terminology has been developed to help people express their rejection or acceptance of the new mix of woe and wealth. Opponents declare, "NIMBY" ("Not in my back yard!"), while others might proclaim "PROWL" ("Please ravish our woeful lawn!"). The new 'moonshiners' are among us.

§ § §

CHAPTER THREE

The Cohorts

The degree of moonshining/bootlegging success that was enjoyed by Prince Farrington was made possible by skilled and loyal cohorts. Briefly, we must mention....

BROTHER "CHARL"

A common, yet picturesque, sight among the rural population of Yesterday's America was the rustic male wearing bib overalls and standing with thumbs caught under the straps. This common pose might be seen wherever rural men were idly standing, such as attending a public sale or chatting with a friend. This was the pose specifically remembered for Lester Seyler (I: 42, etc.) and for Charl Farrington (I: 104-112).

Charles Archibald Farrington and his wife, Virginia Tinsebloom Farrington, came from North Carolina to work with Prince, who bought Charl and Virgie a three-story home on Silver Avenue in Lamar, on the western edge of Clinton County. From here, Charl went forth to do legitimate work as a carpenter. He also gave housing to his family and occasionally, to other kin. At his house in Lamar, Charl hosted parties, complete with juke box music and moonshine liquor. This was also where he made moonshine, sometimes in his basement and sometimes beneath the remains of an old sawmill. From here, Charl – and Virgie on at least one occasion – were taken to jail. The elegant home's unique history is discussed in Chapter Six.

JAKE KOHBERGER

Miller Stamm, of Loganton, characterized the relationship of Prince Farrington and Jake Kohberger as being that of "buddies." Jake, a local native, gave Prince some of his early financial support; a plan from which both benefited nicely. Kohberger helped Prince with his moonshine ventures and apparently did some moonshining of his own. He once owned a store in Carroll but eventually abandoned the store and his marriage. He later ran the *Buffalo Inn* near Jersey Shore; where people could see a small herd of imported bison and eat *buffalo burgers*. These were rarities in a time when few people got to the western part of America and fewer, still, ever saw an American Bison. He later owned a nightclub, the *Minnequa Club*, across the Susquehanna River from Williamsport. All remnants of his businesses are now gone, except for the last house in which he lived.

While Kohberger still operated his store in Carroll, his presence left a lingering impression on Walter Overdorf (See Overdorf's account of a visit to Charl Farrington's house in Chapter Six). Young Walter's parents and grandparents farmed in the area of Tylersville. Once, when his father was going to Kohberger's store in Carroll, Walter was a passenger. He recalls his dad driving the 1927 Chevrolet car. He also recalls that his dad carried a spare axle, since the car "was always breaking down." Once arriving at the store, Walter remained in the car, fascinated with the bobcat that stalked in the cage on the porch of the store. Beside the cage sat a Syracuse Walking Plow. Overdorf's bought the plough. Then Jake Kohberger helped Walter's dad and granddad tie the plow to the back of the car. Jake also loaded a gallon of moonshine into the back seat with Walter. Walter's dad then told him that the plow, and the moonshine, cost a total of $27.00.

Later, when Kohberger owned the *Buffalo Inn*, near Jersey Shore, he had a caged bear, "Inky," as well as the bison herd. One young Kohberger employee was Craig Keen, who pumped gas at the *Buffalo Inn*. One of Keen's strongest impressions was of a time when Kohberger pulled into a gas pump to have his pickup truck fueled. Keen filled the truck, cleaned the windshield and asked if he wanted the oil checked. Then he went into the gas station. Kohberger soon entered the gas station to complain that his windshield was still dirty. Keen returned to the truck and cleaned the windshield another time. Again, Kohberger came back into the station to complain. This time, the impatient employee, told Kohberger, "You're right; but the dirt is on the inside of the windshield and we just cleaned the outside." Jake stared at Keen for a moment and then said, "Son, I think I like you." Then, Craig Keen, remembers, "We got along fine after that."

Keen got to see more of the Kohberger personality than many of his clients. He relates, "When the tenants who lived in the apartments at the inn would get rid of their old clothing or shoes, Jake would sort through the discarded items and, if there was any wear left on the shoes that fit him, Jake would be the new owner of the shoes."

JOE GARDNER

Joe Gardner had a picture hanging in his Lock Haven parlor for many years. The sharp old photograph depicted a moonshining operation at some undisclosed and unrecognizable woodland site. The overall size of the picture slightly exceeds 10" x 13". The photograph reveals piles of kegs, barrels and giant wooden bins, sitting in the vicinity of a couple of large tents and a lean-to type of shelter that protected a large still. Posing amid all the moonshiners' paraphernalia are three men. The middle figure, too professionally dressed for this setting, is Joe Gardner, Prince Farrington's close friend. Prince Farrington would be furious about his outlaw cohorts posing for pictures. No matter. The men sometimes let their likenesses be recorded, thankfully for those of us, today, who wish we could have been witness to some of those unfolding events.

Joe Gardner, a native of Oakdale, North Carolina, came north with his wife, Clara, to work with Prince. He quickly became fully acclimated to Clinton County. He owned farmland and a trucking business and was much involved in community activities. Meanwhile, his brother, George Gardner, married Charl Farrington's daughter, Frances.

Wayne Feerrar has nine aunts and uncles who were sisters-in law and brothers-in-law of Joe Gardner, making Wayne a proud nephew. Wayne notes that, "They were all reluctant to have their names mentioned; but they all indicated that they knew Prince; but with little personal contact with him. They all have high regard for Uncle Joe. He was always helpful and generous to the family and many others... personally or in business."

Joe owned a legitimate business; Lycoming Ash and Garbage Company of Williamsport. June Kreamer Fleisher of Greenburr was his secretary and office manager. They fell in love. His marriage ended and in 1938 he and June were married. The newlyweds lived near the *Florida Fruit Farm* for sometime before moving into Lock Haven. Although he sold his business in Williamsport, he still operated a trucking business until he retired. Gardner also became very active in the community, with membership in several organizations. (It might be noted here, that Prince Farrington is remembered for several direct contributions to the community; but was not so involved as Gardner in community organizations.

However, it is known that Farrington was once a member of the Elks Club of Jersey Shore.)

Joe Gardner's nephew, Wayne Feerrar, lives in Avis. Joe's second wife, June was Wayne Feerrar's aunt through his mother. When June died, it was Wayne Feerrar who settled their estate. That's why he owns the excellent photograph mentioned in Chapter Six. He also has a picture from about 1924 that shows his Uncle Joe, Joe's son, Neese, and another gentleman: Prince Farrington. Joe and his brother had a week's vacation in Florida as young men. The Feerrar brothers came home from Florida with their Aunt June and Uncle Joe. In the Greensboro area of North Carolina, Joe pointed out to his passengers several 'still' sites that he remembered from his youthful days as a Tarheel moonshiner. Wayne's impression of the aging moonshiner/bootlegger? He quickly affirmed that Joe Gardner was "a true southern gentleman."

HENRY SAMPSON

Henry Sampson (1882-1946) came from the Saginaw Chippewa tribe that lived along Saginaw Bay on Lake Huron. He was one of the thousands of Native Americans who came to Cumberland County in Pennsylvania to attend the noted Indian Industrial School, now popularly known as the Carlisle Indian School. Some strange twist of fate brought Farrington and Sampson together and they were friends for years, with Henry bagging potatoes, tending stills and getting tipsy. There was the account (I: 119-120) of Henry showing up, half frozen, at a house in Jersey Shore, because no one came to the still to bring him food or relief from his work. A similar story is told by John Muthler, who says that the same Henry Sampson arrived at the home of Muthler's family one night, intoxicated, and trying to get to Prince's house. Muthler gently sent him to the right house. There was also an account given to this author that the hapless Chippewa did not simply die as the result of falling off a wagon while working, near Salona, for Joe Gardner (I: 118). The version recently told to the author said that two brothers were working with Henry Sampson. As the brothers navigated the full wagon into the barn, with Henry on top of the hay, they seemed to have intentionally rushed directly into the barn, with no chance for Henry to get off or even duck his head. With no time to react, Henry's head struck the door frame and threw him to the ground. Whether by an act of cruel disregard or simply a tumble from a wagon, the graduate of the Carlisle Indian School, now paralyzed, was visited by a sympathetic friend, Prince Farrington. Sampson died several days later. There was no inquest.

THE FLOUNDERING BARRISTER

No one can avoid all of life's pitfalls, no matter how 'distinguished' his life. Attorney John Crawford Youngman, Sr., underwent one of those humiliating episodes. John Crawford Youngman, Sr., had a distinguished career in his legal profession and in his community. His community was primarily Lycoming County. He was born in Williamsport on January 23, 1903, a descendant of Colonel John Henry Antes, for whom Antes Fort, and Antes Creek, are named. One of John Youngman's ancestors was the son-in-law of the pioneer, Colonel Antes. Youngman was, for some years, the county's district attorney. He practiced law into his eighties; but he is best remembered for his opposition to capital punishment, his staunch support of the fluoridation of the city's water supply and his long, and successful effort to have a flood dike created to protect the city from the ravages of a sometimes-errant Susquehanna River. Louis E. Hunsinger's tribute to the man, in an early 2000 historical piece (Williamsport *Sun-Gazette,* "Lycoming County History Makers,") characterized Youngman as being a 'visionary'. The article also shows the private man; the one who loved the outdoors, including fly fishing in Antes Creek.

Two of Pennsylvania's most unique geological oddities are in the fertile Nippenose Valley. There one can find a cluster of deep sinkholes and a related mammoth spring that bubbles forth to become the primary source of Antes Creek. Much of the land through which Antes Creek flows has been owned by Youngman family members. Antes Creek has been touted, since the 19th century, as an excellent stream for fly fishing for trout. Although John C. Youngman fished in relatively placid waters, his family history included a horrific tragedy. 1889 saw torrential rains in the area. The downpour created a flash flood that sent the churning waters of Antes Creek sweeping downstream and ripping away the houses of two Youngman brothers and carrying away the two wives, five children and two other women. Most of the nine people who drowned were ancestors of John Crawford Youngman, who was born about fourteen years after the tragedy.

Attorney Youngman owned a cabin by Antes Creek. He fished alone, sending his line undulating over the waters. One day he lost his balance and fell. With his boots suddenly full of water and the stream waters pushing at his struggling bulk, he was unable to regain his balance and return to a standing position. Simply stated, the former D.A. of the county was losing a battle with the stream of his ancestors.

Happenstance is an informal term first used, it is believed, about 1897. The word signifies something that is a purely chance happening. Happenstance, for Mr. Youngman on that day, was the approach of two boys who realized the lawyer's predicament. They rushed to his aid and helped to steady him and guide him from the stream. They assisted his return to his nearby cabin and got him his dry clothes. They also got him a shot of whiskey from a bottle on a shelf. They probably did what any good Samaritan would have done. Still, when they recounted their help for the floundering Mr. Youngman, their grandmother jokingly chided them, "You should have let him drown! He's the one that put your grandpa in jail!"

THE SEGRAVES SAGA

These were not fictitious given names. Farrington's first name was actually *Prince* and Segraves given name was actually *Colonel*. Colonel Segraves came to Lycoming County from North Carolina and had a traceable family history going back about 1,000 years to England.

The name of Segraves (might also be spelled as *Seagraves*) seems to have been associated with the arrival, in England, of William of Normandy (William, "the Conqueror") in 1066. When William, as King William I of England, ordered an accounting of people, livestock, etc. for purposes of taxation and control, the resulting record became known as The Domesday (pronounced DOOMS day) Book (1086). That record listed the name Segraves in the Leicestershire area. Family research suggests that the Segraves, coming from England and Ireland, may have settled in America as early as the 1690s. During the 1700s, Segraves were living in several states, including North Carolina. Within the Tarheel state, Segraves were soon found in several counties, including Wilkes County.

Colonel Segraves line is easily traced back to a Rev. William Segraves and beyond; but is most manageable if begun, here, with the reverend. Rev. William Segraves was an ex-Confederate soldier who was, in civilian life, a farmer-preacher. Although of an uncertain birthdate, he married Louvenia Elizabeth Creekmore in 1847. Their second son was John Green Segraves (b. 1849), a 19th century distiller of corn whiskey and apple brandy. John Green Segraves was the direct ancestor of Colonel Segraves. Louvenia died at the age of 33 years, leaving a widower and eight children. Within months, Reverend William Segraves had a second wife; a 20-year-old bride, who was already a mother of eight by proxy. The second Mrs. Segraves was Eliza Jane Money (b. 8-8-1839). By the time that she stopped bearing children, at age 41, she had borne another ten children. During her two decades of marriage, then, she was pregnant for approximately 7½ years. The large quantity of kids did not prevent the Revenend and Mrs. Segraves from hosting groups of church members in their modest home, which was situated at the foot of Segraves Mountain in Wilkes County, North Carolina. Colonel Monte Segraves was born September 18, 1909, in Wilkes County, North Carolina. This is the same county that was the birthplace of the celebrated racing driver, Junior Johnson.

Colonel M. Segraves found his bride after moving north into Pennsylvania. His wife was Marie Cathern Engel. They were married in Hagerstown, Maryland. Marie's father, and mother were Anthony and Lucy Eck Engel. The Engels owned a farm above the church and near the town of Bastress. The farm was just off Jack's Hollow Road and had a stream that disappeared into a heavily wooded area, unnoticed by outsiders. The still that Colonel Segraves operated for Prince, was located in an isolated glade on his father-in-law's farm. That still is further identified in Chapter Seven. Colonel Segraves, who was also an able electrician, and his wife moved into Jersey Shore. Soon after their son, James, was born, there was an incident that is still a story within the family. Marie Segraves left tiny James in the care of his father while she attended religious services. The moonshiner and a couple of his friends were the designated baby sitters for the church-going mother. Marie returned to an enlightening scene. Papers were scattered on the table, on which the infant, James, was lying. Fellow moonshiner, Torrence "Diz" Decker was trying to keep the baby steady while the moonshiner father, Colonel Segraves was attempting to pin on a fresh diaper. Revenuers posed a lesser challenge.

Colonel Segraves' wife, Marie Engel Segraves, gives the impression of having been a naturally pleasant woman, quickly seeing humor in unfolding events. She noticed the humor of her grandsons' rescue of the man who put her husband behind bars, and the humor of some tough bootleggers shrinking from a routine diaper change. Also, Marie Engel Segraves could accept, with grace, the illegal nature of her husband's secondary profession.

Despite an almost unblemished arrest record, Colonel Segraves did encounter the law. Although his actual *moonshining* never led to his arrest, Colonel Segraves was apprehended while *peddling* moonshine among some Williamsport customers. For this the Colonel spent six months in the now-obsolete stone prison on Third Street in Williamsport. The prosecuting attorney was John Crawford Youngman, Sr. It was to this sentencing that Marie Segraves, years later, was referring when her grandson, James Segraves II and her step-grandson Kelly Segraves, pulled a cold and water-logged attorney from Antes Creek.

Prince Farrington wasn't the only one of his crowd to get involved in defense work during World War II. Prince, as noted, worked at the ordinance works northwest of Allenwood. Colonel Segraves began working on a super-secret defense project in Tennessee.

Today, the *Oak Ridge Boys*, a country-style vocal group, may be better known; but among the older folks, or among many with a modest sense of history, the name, *Oak Ridge*, has a chilling ring. That is the name of the place that gave birth to the Nuclear Age; the 'town' within which the world's first atomic bomb was fashioned. Oak Ridge is in the Appalachian Mountains, in eastern Tennessee, about 20 miles due west of Knoxville. Seventy-five thousand people were secretly imported to the small city created almost overnight and without appearing on maps. This totally new metropolis was part of a massive program successfully designed to secretly manufacture the "enriched uranium" required to build the atomic bomb.

Several other similarly clandestine sites were established to do certain steps in the process. For example, a laboratory was working beneath the football stadium of the University of Chicago. That laboratory was also working on a critical step in the atomic process. It was there (12/2/42) that Enrico Fermi initiated the world's first nuclear chain reaction. Of course, the secrecy of that small laboratory was much easier to keep, particularly since no one stills hears about that school, even during the height of the college football season.

As a worker at Oak Ridge, Colonel Segraves, an able electrician, worked as a welder. Because of the nature of this classified project, Segraves lived in one valley and traveled through a tunnel to the work site in a neighboring valley. Since the end of the Second World War, the war-created town of Oak Ridge has remained as a normal, small city of about 27,000 people. When Segraves work in Oak Ridge ended, he returned to Williamsport. Later he remarried and was living in New Stanton, Pennsylvania at the time of his death in 1980.

"PUD" HILL: THE MAN FROM THE MOUTH OF PINE CREEK

Dewitt Bodine "Pud" Hill would likely have remained unknown and unmentioned in this book, except for the widespread circulation of an old picture of four moonshiners standing in front of their tent at some remote still. It seemed fitting that the picture should grace the cover of this book, the companion volume to *Prohibition's Prince*. This one had to be entitled: *Prince and the Paupers*. The quartet of petty criminals shown has been identified inside the front cover. They were, from left to right: "Pud" Hill, Lemuel Groce, Charl Farrington and Colonel Segraves. While the hooch that they were peddling could cause occasional agony for the drinkers and their families, this foursome was, otherwise, rather harmless.

In the days when milk was delivered in glass jars, to people's doorstep or to the end of their rural lanes, Hill was a milkman. Some suspected that his milk route was a cover for his moonshine sales. A one-time neighbor recalled nothing connecting "Pud" Hill to moonshining; but that neighbor only remembered Hill when the former moonshiner was older and was frequently seen driving a small, gray 1934 pickup truck or sitting in his front lawn, facing the road, tobacco juice dribbling down the creases of his chin, while reading a 'western'. Unless one is offended by the tobacco juice image, there was nothing recalled about the one-time moonshiner that was particularly negative. The dairy farm on which he lived was in the bottomlands near the mouth of Pine Creek. This is Porter Township, Lycoming Township. "Pud" Hill's wife's name was Eva. A local milk customer also remembers something else about farmer Hill. His milk was priced at eight cents a quart.

When, "Pud" Hill died in 1955, he was buried in the cemetery at Jersey Shore. His gravestone revealed a modest fact that "Pud" hadn't bothered to reveal to acquaintances, or friends, for all his years of contact with many members of the community. Virtually everyone knew "Pud" only by his nickname. Friends and neighbors only knew him as "Pud." While Richard Grugan spent his childhood on the neighboring farm, he never learned "Pud" Hill's given name. Grugan clearly recalls the pleasure he had whenever he encountered his farmer-neighbor, because "Pud" would always give him peppermint candy. Grugan also recalled the day when he and his dad stopped to speak with "Pud" and they heard "Pud" suddenly swear and exclaim, "Oh my God, Mr. Grugan, your barn's on fire!" To be sure! The fire consumed the barn and everything within! Yet, despite Richard Grugan's vivid memories, he still never learned his neighbor's given name.

In 2011, over a half-century after Hill's death, Rick Shaffer, and his wife, Chris, delivered Memorial Day floral arrangements to the local cemetery. They also took the time to locate and read "Pud" Hill's tombstone inscription. Thanks to their effort, we now know that "Pud" Hill carried the given name of DeWitt. His name matched that of the 19th century governor of New York state, DeWitt Clinton. DeWitt Clinton is historically significant for pushing the great Erie Canal project that linked Albany to Lake Ontario. It was Governor DeWitt Clinton whose name is believed to have been attached to Clinton County (founded in 1839, just 14 years after the historic Erie Canal was completed). Clinton County sits just a few yards from the late DeWitt "Pud" Hill's farm home near Jersey Shore.

BOYD "DUKE" GREAK

Dave Berfield is a resident of Bainbridge Island, near Seattle, Washington. He writes of childhood memories that included having a grandmother who "was very much against drink and no alcohol was ever allowed in their house." Dave's mother spoke to him of overhearing her parents (Edgar and Edith Weaver Miller) "talking in whispered tones about a relative that worked for Prince Farrington. I am sure this did not please them." He is now sure that his grandparents were speaking about their nephew, Boyd Greak.

Who was this man, Boyd Greak, who caused relatives to whisper of his exploits? It seems likely that they were discussing Boyd at the time that he was working for Prince and not later when he apparently cut all ties to moonshining and was living a life far different than that of his early years. They were likely discussing the man at the time that he was shot by a revenue agent. As one might express it in today's television phraseology, Boyd Greak took one for Prince. That is, he took a non-fatal bullet in the back while tending one of Prince Farrington's stills on Harbach (Harbaugh) Road, a few yards off Rockey Road, in southern Clinton County.

Boyd "Duke" Greak was born in 1906 in the little crossroads town of Rote, on Route 477, north of Loganton and about ten miles west of the spot where he was wounded. He was a hunter and a fisherman who could get lyrical about nature. He is quoted by an adoring daughter, Barbara (now Clark), as offering this observation on the beauty of a tree:

> "In the spring when the leaves come out they are beautiful and they give you shade. In the fall the leaves turn beautiful colors and they leave the trees because the sap goes down to the roots. Then winter comes and the tree stand in all its glory, waiting for God to bring the sap up the trees to bring forth their new leaves."

When Boyd Greak was a young man, courting Eleanor Sheela, a woman, five years his junior, the distance was daunting for a young man with no automobile. So, for winter courting, he put on ice skates on the river bank at Lock Haven and skated downstream on that great riverine highway, the West Branch of the Susquehanna. About 25 miles later, he arrived at Newberry, near Williamsport. Once at Eleanor's home, she and her beau were allowed to visit in the formal living room. Boyd had no one at home to wash his clothes, so his future mother-in-law would wash them. Since he could not stay in the house overnight, he was given old newspapers to use for bedding. He then went to Memorial Park and slept on a park bench in order to extend his courting of Eleanor into another day.

Boyd, "Duke" Greak had known the smell of sour mash cooking among the shrubs and trees beside the waters of Gann Run. This was just off Rockey Road, on Harbaugh (Harbach) road. He had once worked a still at that site for Prince Farrington. This employment brought "Duke" into that unfortunate situation (I: 97). Prince had numerous stills in operation; but Greak happened to be watching one that was destined to be raided by revenue agents. The sudden attack on this still site sent Greak running into the trees. Then he realized that the pressure building in the heated boiler could cause an explosion. He rushed in, cut the pressure and fled once more; but he couldn't outrun an agent's bullet! He was shot in the back, midway between the heart and spine. Had the bullet's trajectory been an inch or two off to either side, the wound would have been crippling or fatal.

Years passed, Boyd and Eleanor were wed, and Eleanor forbade the mention of any connections that "Duke" ever had with Prince Farrington. The very name, "Duke," that someone had given Boyd Greak years earlier, as a nickname associated with "Prince," was used by all who knew Greak except his wife, Eleanor. His daughter, Barbara, declares, "Daddy and I used to be together a lot." So it was a revelation for Barbara to have an old man ask her, years later at a public event, if she was Boyd Greak's daughter. That stranger proceeded to tell her much that she'd not known. The stranger's belated "news" helped to explain the "hole" that she had seen in her dad's back, from a decades'-old wound left by a government bullet. Despite the injury, and the deep wound that remained, Boyd "Duke" Greak reached the octogenarian plateau before his 1989 demise.

Here is an unrelated quote from a cousin of Boyd Greak, Mr. Dave Berfield of Bainbridge Island, Washington. As a youngster he lived in Jersey Shore, close to the stream that flows just west of the town and intersects with the Susquehanna River. Berfield writes of a phrase that he had heard, "If you dip your feet in Pine Creek, your heart will never leave. I think that is true." He would know.

An afterthought: If one looks closely at the main characters in the Farrington Saga, an interesting conclusion can be drawn. Talking with many people about the likes of Boyd Greak, DeWitt Hill, Charl Farrington, Joe Gardner, George Gardner, Colonel Segraves, Jake Kohberger, Turburt Seyler, Walt Wagner, Charles Klobe, Floyd Klobe, Herman Klobe, and, yes, even Prince Farrington himself, it becomes obvious that these were not the personalities that one encounters in the Prohibition tales of the large American cities. Here, in the Pennsylvania hinterlands, people made their own alcohol without fear of retribution from the bigger players. There was no gangland violence and no gunning to death of rivals. Clinton and Lycoming counties experienced considerable moonshining and bootlegging; but, when it all ended, primarily with the death in 1956, of Prince David Farrington, moonshining had already become an obsolete way of making and marketing alcohol.

CHAPTER FOUR

Other Major Players

YOUNG COLTRANE

B. W. Coltrane (I:70-71, etc.) was Prince Farrington's nephew, who had come to Pennsylvania from North Carolina with his parents and a brother. He told few people his real name; but one of those was his close friend, Leo "Chip" Taylor, from whom we learned that the B. W. was for Batie Worth. He helped Prince in the moonshining business. Through the voices of Fran Bailey Grugan, Tom Bauman, and the late Leo "Chip" Taylor, we get a picture of a pleasant young man who helped Prince tally his moonshine output, etc. and who helped build Prince's image by being, himself, a charming young man. Fran Bailey Grugan was the daughter of Leslie Bailey, who managed the service station in Antes Fort at one time. Fran remembers B. W. Coltrane (I: 70-71, etc.) as a very pleasant boarder in their house when she was a young teen. She also offered a couple of pictures of B. W. that were snapped when he was in the military. A verbal glimpse of Batie Worth Coltrane came from Leo "Chip" Taylor who spoke of a time when B. W. was an older man, returning to the area for a visit. The Taylors went to the *Antiques Inn* with B. W. and B. W.'s lady friend. B. W. Coltrane, by most accounts, was admired by many who came into his presence, as a fine looking and personable man; but this evening, his lady companion walked out of the tavern, offended by Coltrane's heavy drinking. B. W. Coltrane seemed to have joined the growing number of Prince's relatives who had become overly dependent on their own product.

A LIKABLE YOUNG MAN

Prince had a nephew named Lobby Anthony, the son of Prince's brother-in-law, Scott Anthony of Greensboro, North Carolina. Lobby, too, travelled north to visit with Prince's family. Tom Bauman, the neighbor of Prince, who visited often, happened to be there on a winter day when Whitey (Prince, Jr.) was planning to go out on the following morning to check his trap line to see if he had caught any muskrats, skunks, raccoon or some other varmints. Tom Bauman and Lobby Anthony agreed to help Whitey. As it happened, Lobby had brought a pair of boots; but they were too short, while Tom Bauman's boots, which had been given to him, were too large. They swapped boots and seemed to become friends in the trade. The following day they began their long upstream walk on the bank of the Susquehanna River. Whitey's traps had garnered four or five muskrats and, Tom recalled, a raccoon. Bauman also recalled that it was very cold; but Lobby seemed comfortable in a wool shirt, a leather jacket, and no hat! Bauman was suffering from cold hands, from helping check the animals and traps in the cold river water. Lobby then gave Tom the gloves he had been wearing. They were leather and lined with rabbit fur. Lobby said, "Here, these will keep your hands warm." It was a gesture to be remembered for a lifetime. Bauman explained, "We kidded each other about trading boots, and I got to like him. He was just the sort of guy you could like. There was nothing phony about him."

Bauman had another memory to share. "The following year Whitey and I had been down at the farm and were walking up to the house. Gladys and George (Porter) had been living in the brick house with Prince. While we were walking toward the house, we came to three ox heart cherry trees. It comes to my mind that they were on Muthler's ground (a neighboring farmer); but we climbed into one of the trees. The cherries weren't quite ripe; but we ate a few. We got down out of the tree and here comes Gladys in a car. When she pulled up where we were, she was crying. Whitey asked, "What's the matter?" and she said, "Lobby was killed in a car wreck last night!"

"HOP"

He was the youngest of Prince's siblings and the one who took the use of alcohol beyond the outer limits. George Hobson Farrington was known as "Hop." The family says that young George Hobson Farrington had such frightening attacks of the delirium tremens that they had a physician summoned. The physician, the family laments, gave him a shot to stop the attack; but it killed the patient. There is no evidence that "Hop" Farrington's tragic death had any impact on other family members, regarding abandoning their pursuit of alcohol. However, one family friend may have been shocked out of any interest in "demon rum," as alcohol was disparagingly described. Tom Bauman tells of visiting Whitey and Gayle at Prince's house. "Hop" was also there. The alcoholic was leaving one room, through the parlor doors. He had just opened the doors when he went into a delirious fit! He screamed, "Don't let them get me." He was screaming and thrashing about, totally out of control, because of his delirium tremens. Bauman was totally unnerved. Prince's middle son, Gayle, was a husky young man who was finally able to get "Hop" under control. Aside from "Hop's" severe alcoholic condition, what triggered his delirious outburst? It happened because, as he opened the parlor doors, he was suddenly confronted by a stranger! The stranger was actually the newel post of the stair railing, topped with Prince's coat and his hat!

Bauman's reflection: "To this day I think seeing "Hop" like that, when I was just a kid, kind of made me ask, 'What in the hell does somebody use that stuff for?' You know, they don't make you drink it. I never had trouble with booze." In 1951 Tom Bauman, the non-drinker, also quit smoking. Six decades later, he remains free of both habits.

RAY WYNN

Ray Wynn was typical of some of the local people who worked for Prince Farrington. Wynn was a farmer who did some moonlighting by making moonshine. His farming was done with a 1938 Farmall F14, which was modified to hold rims and ties. Ray Wynn did many other things, all legal, to increase his income and decrease his food bill, as mentioned in Chapter Two. The one illegal thing that he did was to work stills at night for Prince. He got caught and put into the Clinton County jail for 30 days; but not for 30 nights! His stay was made somewhat less difficult by Sheriff George Hickoff, who would allow Wynn to go home at night, with the sheriff even delivering Wynn to his family. Ray Wynn also stored liquor for Prince. Prince especially liked Ray because none of the stored liquor was ever missing. Ray was married to a Welshans, linking the Wynn family to one of the historic families of Nippenose Valley. Ray's son, Art Wynn, worked for Jake Kohberger.

"FUZZ"

Another local man, Harry "Fuzz" Shaffer, worked for Prince until, after his divorce, he moved to New York State and got a job with the Ingersoll-Rand Corporation. Eventually, the locals say, he became the head of Ingersoll-Rands security department.

TURBERT SEYLER

Turbert Seyler worked for Prince Farrington. They lived as neighbors in the early days of Prince's work in Pennsylvania. Liquor agents tried to catch Seyler with alcohol. One effort they made was to stop Seyler just north of Loganton, near the sulpher spring that sits beside the highway outside of town. The children's presence in the car didn't deter the authorities. They stopped Seyler and had his children climb from the car. Then they pulled out the seats. There was no alcohol to be found.

Seyler's son-in-law was Walt Wagner. He and the family lived in an old log house. Today the house where they lived no longer exists. It was removed when the reservoir was built for the collecting of water for Lock Haven's municipal water supply. Did Walt Wagner work for Prince? No, says his son, John. Walt made his own. The Wagners lived in one side only. The other side housed Walt's special guests: a still and the large mash boxes. John Wagner reminds the listener that a number of people in the area were making their own moonshine. In their case, John tells us, it was a vital part of the family income.

THE CURIOUS COLONEL

We remember some people's lives because things that happened to them were interesting, such as being a survivor of the Bataan "Death March" during World War II or being witness to the Hindenburg airship tragedy in Lakehurst, New Jersey in 1937. Others are remembered because the individuals, themselves, were unique. Prince Farrington would be among the latter. So was Colonel Henry Shoemaker (I: 122). Prince Farrington had a handful of truly interesting friends or acquaintances; but the strangest man to cross paths with Prince Farrington was a man whose prominence far exceeded that of Prince Farrington during Prince's lifetime and since. This man was Colonel Henry Wharton Shoemaker (1880-1958), who was widely known throughout the state of Pennsylvania and who was also known beyond the Keystone State.

Despite much focus on his association with his home, "Restless Oaks," in McElhattan (Clinton County, Pennsylvania), Colonel Shoemaker was among the most cosmopolitan men of his time. He spent much of his lifetime in other counties, other states and other nations. His Wikipedia biographical sketch tells us that he spent several childhood summers in India, studied at Columbia University in New York City, published newspapers in three Pennsylvania municipalities, Reading, Altoona and Jersey Shore (Clinton County) and worked in a number of European embassies. He was also a U.S. ambassador to Bulgaria. He was a campaign writer for Gifford Pinchot in Pinchot's runs for the U.S. Senate and the state's governorship. He also was a state chairperson for Herbert Hoover's 1929 campaign for U.S. president. His political ties got him a half-dozen appointed positions in Harrisburg.

Colonel Henry Wharton Shoemaker also had several connections with Prince Farrington. The distance between their homes – McElhattan for Shoemaker and Antes Fort for Farrington – was less than ten miles. They had become good friends; perhaps because Prince loved to make and sell moonshine and because the colonel loved to buy and drink the same concoction. Shoemaker had influence in places that Prince could not have hoped to breach without someone else's calling card. Prince's family has suggested that they felt that it was Shoemaker who got Clinton and Lycoming County moonshine into the halls of both our state and our national capitols. As we learn more about the veracity of the man from McElhattan, a question might be posed: Was Colonel Henry Wharton Shoemaker's output of tales fueled more by Farrington moonshine than by factual sources? The folklorist was, himself, a participant in one of the area's most fascinating new folk tales; the legend of Prince Farrington.

Colonel Shoemaker was born to wealth; but his enduring fame was the result of his writings, many of which were folk tales about the early frontier of central Pennsylvania. Unfortunately for Shoemaker, a few people insisted on knowing the sources of his stories, when he had no sources to offer. Also, unfortunately, most people accepted his stories as authentic, thus allowing Shoemaker to gain in fame and sales of his spurious tales. It must also be observed that phony history is often repeated by others, thus spreading the phoniness. (It should be noted that H. L. Mencken once wrote a satirical article about bathtubs. It was not meant to be taken seriously; but it was quoted in numerous articles by several undiscerning authors. Other dishonest accounts have been repeatedly borrowed by serious scholars.)

Even as recently as the 1990s, a book reviewer for the *Carnegie Magazine*, Ellen S. Wilson, was lavishing praise on the late literary hustler from McElhattan. Ms. Wilson even elevated her subject's character to the point of saying that Shoemaker had a vision of "the moral value of the natural world," and that "the vision that led him to conserve the old stories was strong." She also noted that Shoemaker had written 4,000 of those roadside historical markers. If she is referring to Pennsylvania's official state markers, the number barely exceeds 2,600, many of which were inspired by other individuals and groups. She, too, seemed to subscribe to the notion that people were off-handedly condemning his collecting of folk tales. Ms. Wilson, and many others don't face a basic question: Did he *collect* stories or did he simply *fabricate* stories, or did he do both? Until that information is established, evaluations of his work shouldn't be undertaken. It wasn't his *collecting* of authentic folk tales that was earning condemnation for the

Colonel; but his *willingness to fabricate entire stories that were patently baseless and then allowing readers to think that they were honoring events of the past when they were merely honoring Shoemaker's unbridled imagination.* His literary fraudulence was then compounded when he encouraged monuments to characters that he had manufactured. Let's be grateful for the debunkers.

THE DEBUNKERS

A debunker is one who exposes the fraudulent and the dishonest. The debunkers expose the scams that plague our present-day society. The debunker should be among the few people in our society to be placed on a pedestal. We need people who can be trusted to "tell it like it is," to use a slangy modern phrase. Here are a few of the debunkers who have helped to expose Colonel Henry Shoemaker's perverted history.

William S. Hunter was a state historian who told the author (about 1970) that when some of Colonel Shoemaker's best accounts were questioned, he'd typically say that he was talking with someone in a tavern somewhere and had no written or taped record.

Billy Mattern of Mifflinburg wrote the monograph cited in *Prohibition's Prince* (I:122; 256) that demolished the fabrication about the destruction of the last herd of Buffalo in the state, despite the belief that Pennsylvania, without expanses of great grassy prairies, has never had buffalo herds.

Norman Houser is among Colonel Henry W. Shoemaker's most recent debunkers. Houser maintains an internet blog: "The Pennsylvania Rambler." His evaluation of Shoemaker is blunt: The man from McElhattan was "noted for making up his own legends and stories about Central Pennslvania." Houser, in separate blogs, cites three specific legends by Shoemaker. One (Blog date: 2/27/10) tells of a woman's ghost that roams toward an eternal destination in the Black Moshannon State Park (Centre County). A second Shoemaker tale (Blog date 5/22/10) involves the Moshannon Creek, also in Centre County. This tale describes an ancient fortress with semi-circular walls about eight feet in height and with a diameter of 800 feet. In near proximity to these fortress ruins were seven blood-stained stone pillars about six feet tall. As with many a literary hoax, this one appeared in newspapers from time to time as historical fact rather than just one more Shoemaker sham.

The third of Houser's anti-Shoemaker blogs is the one (3/12/10) about a tale that must be true: It is writ in stone! The account of Captain Harry Green and his companions informed readers that a Captain Green and four other frontiersmen pursued Indian renegades from the Juniata County area to Sugar Valley (Clinton

County), where the Indians doubled back and massacred their five pursuers. With the cooperation of Shoemaker, the storyteller, a stone pillar encasing a stone plaque was built in 1916 at Carroll, just off what is now the Interstate 80 Jersey Shore exit. Here is the inscription: "One mile south of this marker is the spot reputed by local history as being the scene of a massacre of Captain Harry Green and companions by a band of marauding Indians Feb. 1801. Erected by Col. H. W. Shoemaker, Daniel Mark, A.D. Karstetter, J.W. Zimmerman." Apparently no one, including Norman Houser, has found any evidence of a Harry Green, scalped or alive. This has led Houser to conclude his related blog by observing, "As I read who erected the monument, I see the name of Colonel Henry Shoemaker... Suddenly the possibility of this actually happening slips to a one in a million chance. Shoemaker's record of being truthful is up in the air as more and more research on him is done."

There is a Penn State University web site writer who addresses a lone Shoemaker fabrication. By viewing the site (http://www.psu.edu/ur/about/myths.html) the reader can learn the following: "*Princess Nita-nee* was 'invented' by author and publisher Henry W. Shoemaker and has no basis whatever in fact. Shoemaker's mention of the princess first appeared in print in 1903." The Penn State document also tells us that Shoemaker later admitted that the name, 'Nita-nee', was "purely fictitious.'"

A MAN OF *LETTERS*?

Much depth is added to the Shoemaker profile by **Gloria Schadt Harbach**, formerly of Castanea and now a resident of Williamsport. Her observations take on a special quality because she is a distant relative of the curious colonel. Their common ancestor was John George Shoemaker, Sr. That relationship means that Gloria Harbach is Colonel Henry Wharton Shoemaker's fourth cousin, thrice removed. She and her husband, Jack Harbach, himself an author, had been unable to find any documentary support for the "Green Massacre." Also, Mrs. Harbach tells us that she perceived an obvious "lack of complimentary remarks about him from my relatives as I grew up." Shoemaker married well. That is to say, he married twice and each bride was from a wealthy family, the daughter of a prominent man of the time. Nuptial vows did not prevent Colonel Shoemaker from fathering several children out of wedlock or having relationships with several mistresses. In fact, Gloria Harbach *owns* enough love letters, from Shoemaker's mistresses, to fill two containers. Having read this author's critical biographical sketch of Henry Shoemaker (*Keystone*, p. 29-30), Ms. Harbach commented, "I'm glad there are people... who see through his gory stories." She also owns one of the folklorist's scrapbooks, in which he gathered a collection of newspaper and magazine pictures of women's legs, many of which were from stocking ads. That isn't folklore...

In May of 1996, Simon Bronner delivered a lecture before the Snyder County (PA) Historical Society (The Snyder County Historical Society Bulletin, 1996, Pages 81-97), in which he cited Shoemaker's 1912 work *Pennsylvania Mountain Stories* and that book's mention of the "Indian Mound" that sits just north of the Union County town of Dice. In the 1970s, this author, with several family members and a geology student from Susquehanna University, visited that 'mound'. By removing a few inches of ground from the surface, it was clear that the mound wasn't erected from 'fill'. It has undisturbed stratification resting on bedrock; a natural geological phenomenon. However, read Shoemaker's eloquent fabrication, properly cited by Professor Bronner (*Eldorado Found*, p. 82): Shoemaker's 'mound' is "a sort of redskin Tower of Babel erected by a proud chieftain of ancient days, which brought only confusion to the Indian ruler and his people."

Despite his busy life of newspaper publishing, politicking and writing, Colonel Shoemaker found time for visits to Prince Farrington's home, in order to replenish his 'fuel' supply. Farrington's son-in-law noted that Shoemaker was "a frequent caller." A symbiotic relationship in nature is where two dissimilar organisms live together for mutual advantage. Prince and the Colonel had such a relationship.

Colonel Shoemaker's political influence far exceeded his historical reliability. Thus, in 1948, he was given another political plum, especially plucked for one with his influence. He was appointed to a newly-created post: *State Folklorist*. Not only was he the first to hold such a position in Pennsylvania; he was the first so honored in the entire country. What had they done? Some in Harrisburg seemed to have second thoughts. The writers who suggest that Colonel Henry Shoemaker's contributions to folklore resulted from his pursuit of some great moral truth, should reflect on their utterances. Any writer who penned laudable observations after about 1980 should have known of Shoemaker's pattern of fabrication and his willingness to deceive his readers. People in Harrisburg were beginning to feel that Shoemaker was minimizing the integrity that should have been underpinning the work of the Pennsylvania Historical and Museum Commission. Other men were designated as state folklorists; but none were given the prominence and influence that Prince Farrington's friend, Colonel Henry Wharton Shoemaker, had enjoyed. The position that first honored Shoemaker was abolished in the 1990s. Thankfully, those who appreciate the authentic treatment of folklore expect more reliable work. One might be amused by the knavery of Shoemaker; but we must take our folklore seriously. Thanks to the Colonel from McElhattan, "Princess Nita-nee" is now free to roam with Paul Bunyan, and "the last buffalo herd in Pennsylvania" is now free to graze beside Bunyan's blue ox, 'Babe'.

§ § §

CHAPTER FIVE

"Moon Shine Farm": The Klobe Clan

A ROBUST FAMILY NEAR CARROLL

The title of this chapter is borrowed from the painted inscription on a stone at one of the early Klobe farmhouses (note the accompanying photograph). That inscription, however, was said to have been painted by the *current* owner of the house, and was not painted by a Klobe family member.

The late Thelma Matthews (I: 63) recalled standing with her husband at their house near Carroll and gazing on the wooded flatlands to the south. There the couple would count columns of smoke; the early-morning evidence of a cluster of hidden, illegal stills on the neighbors' property. Those neighbors were members of the Klobe family. The Klobes, too, knew how to manufacture moonshine.

The patriarch of this family was Herman Henry Klobe, the son of a German immigrant. In 1927, Herman, now partially incapacitated by a stroke, was living with a son, Charles. A second son, Floyd Klobe, lived nearby. The Klobe farms were in Sugar Valley, at the town of Carroll and just about a dozen miles from Prince Farrington's first Pennsylvania home, the *Florida Fruit Farm*.

Regarding the relationship between the moonshiner Farrington and the moonshining Klobe family, George Mayes of Antes Fort (I: 94) was quoted as observing that it was a Klobe who would set up stills for Prince Farrington.

However, one family member insists that Charles "was never affiliated with Prince." Farrington's ties to the Klobes seem to have been with Herman and his younger son, Floyd. Still, another relative says that both Klobes, "Floyd, and brother Charles, made whiskey on their own." There is convincing evidence of that.

Herman also employed a couple of hands, Louis Huntingdon and Earl Knepp to help him with his work, part of which included the making of moonshine whiskey. The tranquility of the eastern end of Sugar Valley was shattered on Tuesday night, August 16th of 1927. On that summer evening, alcohol and a heated argument between Floyd Klobe and Louis Huntingdon led to a violent confrontation between the two. Young Floyd received an ax-related gash that left his cheek scarred for life. The elderly (72-years-old) Herman Klobe, who hadn't been directly involved in the quarrel, wandered onto the scene and, somehow, had his head split by an ax. He died a couple of days later, and the ensuing investigation and trial (I: 95-6) left no clear perpetrator for the grisly crime.

Herman Klobe's two sons, Charles and Floyd, had their own careers in moonshining over the years, even though, for many years, they didn't speak to one another. The 1927 trial of Louis B. Huntingdon, for the murder of Herman Klobe, openly indicated that Herman and both his sons, Charles and Floyd, were involved, at that time, with making illicit whiskey. The trial resulted in the acquittal of Huntingdon. Further, years after the death of Herman Henry Klobe (I: 94), his older son, Charles, told a friend, Ed Pickett, that his father's death was truly accidental. The presence of a sharp, double-bitted ax, firmly implanted into the chopping block was a poor place to be having a drunken quarrel. While the fight was believed to be over money or moonshine, it was primarily between Floyd Klobe and Louis B. Huntingdon. Herman Klobe, also soused, got involved and, Charles insisted, fell onto the ax, with fatal results. Contradicting that, in part, another family member claimed that, away from the courtroom, Huntingdon had admitted his culpability in the heinous act. Apparently, the true story of Herman Klobe's death will remain forever unresolved.

A MAN OF MANY PARTS

If one bases his or her evaluation of Herman Henry Klobe entirely on the sensational newspaper accounts of the trial resulting from his bloody demise, the result would be very warped. One would get the impression of an elderly farmer who spent his entire life tilling the soil and dabbling in moonshine, until the night when he met his doom as the result of a back-country brawl. How distorted a portrait!

Herman Klobe's father was a German immigrant who was married to a member of the Martz family of Eastville, in Sugar Valley. Although the family has few written documents, family tradition is strong. Herman's father was a wealthy industrialist in Philadelphia which was, at the time, one of America's largest, most vibrant cities. Here is where young Herman lived. His mother died when he was a young boy and, when he was still a lad approaching his teen years, his father was murdered and his body dumped into the one of the city's rivers. The crime, the family understands, was done on orders from Klobe's business partner, as a way to gain full ownership of the company. At the age of 12, Herman Henry Klobe was an orphan.

At the time of his death, in 1831, Philadelphia's Stephen Girard was possibly the wealthiest man in America. Girard's will endowed a school, Girard College, that would care for and educate white males who were orphans or whose father was dead. Although Girard College can find no record for Klobe, he appears to have been put in the custody and care of Girard College by the court. His descendants were also aware that Herman Klobe had some natural artistic ability and worked for some time at painting scenes for Philadelphia theaters. There was a negative side to his artistry. The paints of the time caused Klobe to experience respiratory problems. He needed to change his environment.

While still a young man, Herman Klobe returned from the great metropolitan center to the home of his maternal grandparents, the Martz family of Sugar Valley. Although Sugar Valley had a number of sawmills, Klobe found work in a large sawmill in Pine Creek Hollow, near the village of Woodward (Centre County). To get to work – weekly, or whenever – he walked many miles southward and across a couple of mountains. While working at Woodward, Herman Klobe met and courted Margaret Louise Miller. A grandchild still has the bundle of love letters that Klobe wrote to his Penn Valley ladylove. On March 21st of 1889, Herman and Margaret were married. They went to housekeeping in a mountainside house in the eastern end of Sugar Valley.

There is something special about those love letters, aside from the passionate prose. They were adorned with sketches, examples of Herman Henry Klobe's artistic skills. He also painted or did charcoal portraits of local individuals, works several of which are still in existence. Equally fascinating: Herman Klobe would go to the general store in Carroll to sit and sketch customers. Lastly, Klobe's granddaughter, Thelma Bierly, owns what she considers to be a prized art work. It is a charcoal work showing a curly-haired little girl and a similarly curly-haired dog.

A look at one of his letters is valuable in showing the letter-writing style of the times, the stage of their relationship, Herman Klobe's superb penmanship and his artistically self-adorned stationery. The message, given here in full and unmodified, says:

> Pine Creek Hollow, Feb. the 9th 1889
> Dearest and best
> Yours of the 5th instand at hand, I feel very lonesome since you have left, time (?) seems long to me, for instance when Saturday night comes I had bin out on Wednesday evening But you had gone of(f) so I felt dispointed. So I stayed at your folks until 9 Oclock Clody told me that you had told hir that I was to go over to see that woman that told you that I had been married I had a notion to do so being you were gone. I had bin over home last Sunday and brought my close over and now Im ready if (the word 'if" has a line of cancellation through it.) to get married now at anytime if it suits you, and as you say in your letter you trouble yourself Dear you nead not for I'll never dispoint you for I'll be a Man, and your's only Clody had bin telling Me, that you were troubling yourself about something so your Mother said wether I had told you something which you did not like so I told Clody I wouldent know what it could be. But I'll be up if the wheather is nice next Saturday evinning this is all for this time My dearest hoping to have an early reply from you
>
> From Your's forever,
> H.H. Klobe
> Please and address to
> Woodward
> PA

Herman and Margaret had three children. The oldest was Bertha, who became Mrs. Bertha Farmer of New York City. She, too, was an artist and did some painting in that metropolis. She rarely returned to her country roots. Their second child was Charles and the third was Floyd, both of whom are discussed below.

Herman's beloved Margaret died in 1924, so she was no longer in his life on that fateful night of August 16, 1927.

CHARLES LEE KLOBE, SR.

Charles Lee Klobe was the older of the two Klobe boys, having been born August 10th of 1890. He was a native of Sugar Valley, having been born near the town of Carroll. In 1912 he married Margaret ("Maggie") Yarrison. Although his younger brother, Floyd, would father just one child, Charles and Maggie were more prolific. They had eleven offspring. Of their eleven-member brood, only one son, Lindy Herman Klobe, collected a few arrest citations, including (*The Wellsboro Agitator*, 8/16/56) shooting at game from an automobile and hunting while his license was suspended. Those charges were handled when Lindy paid a fine of $90.00 in what was known as a 'field settlement'. Another newspaper report (*The Williamsport Gazette and Bulletin*, 1/28/48) says that Lindy was involved in the theft of sawmill fittings. Lindy may have inherited a genetic defect from his grandfather, since he suffered a stroke, as had his grandfather, Herman. Lindy, more incapacitated than his grandfather, spent years in a wheelchair.

One family member felt strongly that the younger Klobe brother, Floyd, both delivered and stored whiskey for Prince. That person also felt that Charles and Floyd, together, began moonshining when Prince, once again, was sent to prison. Although Floyd was never arrested; Charles Klobe, Sr., was. An undated newspaper clipping from the author's file indicates that Charles Klobe, Sr. was arrested, along with his wife, Margaret, and one son, Willard, when officers raided the still that they were operating at the Tea Spring. The location of the Tea Spring, a natural area, is about five miles east of their home. Officers came prepared. They had the red pepper needed to subdue Klobe's watchdogs. The size of the operation was impressive, according to the newspaper account. Authorities gave the still size as being 750 gallons. They also confiscated 37 gallons of moonshine and more than a thousand gallons of mash. Ed Pickett tells of a conversation he had with Charles Klobe, Sr. in the 1970s, during which Klobe told Pickett of aging his product by burying it in small caves and that he had an old white mule that was used for carrying his moonshining supplies. Despite those confessions, Pickett fondly remembers Charles Klobe, Sr., not so much for his moonshining; but for giving Pickett good advice for catching 'brookies' (brook trout).

Despite the fanfare that seemed to surround the arrest of Charles, Margaret and son Willard, no convictions occurred, so both of Herman Klobe's sons kept an unblemished record as far as convictions were concerned.

Although Charles Lee Klobe, Sr. did some moonshining in his earlier years, he was obviously highly regarded within his community. He was, at the time of his registration for the military draft for World War I, listed as a lineman for the old Western Union Telegraph Company. At another time, he was an engineer for the Bell Telephone Company. Prince Farrington wasn't the only moonshiner who found employment at the Ordinance Depot that swallowed the town of Alvira. Charles Lee Klobe, Sr., also worked at the U.S. government's World War II Ordinance Depot, northwest of Allenwood.

Charles was a member of the Sugar Valley Church of the Brethren, in Eastville. He also farmed, hunted and fished. He was a member of the local branch of the Carpenters Union. In 1957 he also opened a hobby shop and began making apple and potato crates. Maggie and Charles Klobe were chosen as the Loganton's Bicentennial Couple. Then, in 1977, Maggie and Charles were honored as the longest-married couple in Sugar Valley. A few years later, in 1982, when both were ninety years old, Maggie and Charles celebrated their 70th wedding anniversary. She died three years later.

In 1990, Charles Klobe, Sr., was featured in a newspaper (The Lock Haven *Express*) while observing his 100th birthday, celebrated in a Lock Haven nursing facility and surrounded by five of his great-great-grandchildren. His one great-granddaughter had been coming to visit him on his birthday for several years; a real tribute to Klobe, since they lived in Ecuador. Charles Lee Klobe died later that year. Maggie and Charles are buried in the churchyard in Eastville.

Six of Charles and Maggie's children are still living. Willard, 95, lives in Milton. Dorothy Meixel, 91, also lives in Milton, as does Mildred, who is 88. Another daughter, Thelma Bierly, lives in Tylersville and Charles, Jr., lives in Mill Hall where he takes an occasional meal at Aungst's restaurant, where he can chat with the restaurant's manager, Tammy Farrington, who is Prince Farrington's grand-niece. The youngest, Harold Klobe, lives in California. Now retired from a position with United Airlines, he remains on the company's board of directors.

FLOYD CURTIS KLOBE

Floyd Curtis Klobe was born October 3, 1893. He worked on his father's farm and, presumably, learned the techniques needed for productive farming and for successful distilling. Floyd married a young woman from Rockey Road named Thressa S. Rush. Thressa Rush Klobe, who was born in 1903, was likely the most scandalous figure to come out of Sugar Valley.

Thressa's mother was Ida Mae Confer, daughter of Lincoln and Clara Orndorf Confer. Ida, who was born in Loganton in 1882, appears to have had her first child, Thressa, out of wedlock with a man named David Rush. When Ida bore Thressa, in 1903, she had her baby daughter baptized in Loganton's Albright Evangelical Church. According to some accounts, the infant girl's name was listed as Sarah Teresa Rush. Later, Thressa's mother married Adam Stabley.

Adam Harrison Stabley's ancestors were from York County, where Adam was born. Adam is remembered in Sugar Valley for having his own still (I: 48, 91-4) and for operating the *101 Ranch*. That enterprise, the *101 Ranch* was a large house on Rockey Road, close to the farm of Gladys and George Rockey. There was a small, non-bank-type barn on the property. Older residents remember the *101 Ranch* as a business that offered alcohol and women to local patrons. It was also described, by one older resident, as having "booze and big parties." A later generation saw the building become the Chester Kulp property. Still later, the house burned. Today, a mobile home occupies the land once occupied by Adam Stabley's rural enterprise. Adam and Ida Confer Stabley had a small brood of children; at least a half-dozen. In their later years, the Stabley's lived on Allegheny Street in Jersey Shore. Adam preceded Ida in death. Ida – Thressa Rush Klobe's mother – suffered for years from diabetes before her death in 1959.

As a young woman, Thressa left Sugar Valley to become a chorus girl in New York City. When the body of an unidentified, and unidentifiable, young woman was found near Rauchtown (I: 92), in 1925, some people quickly assumed that it was Thressa. They were wrong. Thressa, in good health, reappeared locally many months later.

When Thressa Rush married Floyd Klobe, they moved to the Jersey Shore area. Floyd worked for the railroad. They became parents of a daughter (April 14, 1919), whom they named Ethel. One day Floyd returned from work to find that Thressa had gone back to the city and the chorus line, abandoning him as well as their baby. Thressa had left tiny Ethel reclining in a dresser drawer.

Floyd, although still married, was suddenly a single parent. He quit his railroad job to care for his infant daughter. His brother, Charles, and sister-in-law, Margaret, also helped care for Thressa's abandoned child. Floyd obtained a divorce from Thressa, through the Lycoming County court, on May 26, 1924.

About the time that his daughter, Ethel, was approaching school age, Floyd began a relationship with Etta Long Raudabaugh, a widow whose husband had been killed in the First World War. Although they never married, Etta and Floyd lived together for about a half-century, until Floyd's death in January of 1979. Just as critical, Floyd's mate, Etta, and his daughter, Ethel, considered themselves to be in a true mother/daughter relationship, just as, years later, Ethel's children would also consider Etta to have been their true grandmother. Daughter Ethel was a childhood friend of her cousins, Charles Klobe's children, as well as those of the Carroll storekeeper and moonshiner, Jake Kohberger (I: 120). Years later, Ethel told her own children that it was Etta Raudabaugh's widow's pension that provided their main revenue for years. There was, of course, whatever Floyd Klobe was earning from his distilling of illegal liquor. He also bought the Gottleib Derr farm on Winter Road (the road that stretches through the south side of Sugar Valley). It was on this farm that Floyd Klobe's main still was the one hidden beneath a shed floor; one that could only be accessed through a concealed trapdoor. The rough locations of several of Floyd's stills are identified in Chapter Seven.

As a small child, Ethel was sometimes visited by her mother. Thressa would arrive in a fancy automobile and with expensive dresses for Ethel. Ethel, identified, in the terminology of the time as a 'tomboy', was unimpressed with the clothing and was fearful that her mother would take her away. Sometimes when Thressa would return, Ethel would crawl under the front porch or rush to the attic. She did relate, years later, that she had talked with her mother on a couple of occasions. But, in 1929, Thressa – then in her mid-twenties – was riding with a friend, J. L. "Joe" Hart, in a roadster over Pine Mountain. That road, connecting tiny Pine Station with Rauchtown, has some treacherous turns even today. With Joe driving, the vehicle careened off the road and collided with a tree! Thressa's skull was fractured as she was thrown through the windshield. Her remains were interred in the Mount Pleasant cemetery in Rosecrans. A coroner's jury later absolved Hart of any responsibility for the "death of Miss Tessie Rush." Her daughter, Ethel, was about ten years old.

Floyd Klobe's granddaughter, Beulah Quiggle Neff, felt that the Klobes came to know Prince Farrington through Floyd's ex-wife, Thressa and Mr. and Mrs. Stabley. Prince had lived close to the Stableys when he lived on the *Florida Fruit Farm*. He was an occasional visitor with the Klobes at their home near Carroll and later at their farm. Prince apparently won the admiration of Ethel, the young daughter of Floyd. She told of his visits and of her awareness of his beautiful teeth and of his use of a stick to keep them clean. (Here, again, numerous people commented on the brightness of Prince Farrington's teeth. Tom Bauman, a friend and neighbor of the Farringtons observed, "And when Prince picked his teeth, I don't know. I've had different guys tell me it was a pine stick or birch or something. It wasn't until the last time he was in prison, that he started to have some tooth problems. Up until that time, to the best of my knowledge, he never had any fillings or anything." Another observation by Ethel Klobe was similar to that of several other individuals. She, too, told of noticing that Prince Farrington's complexion was darker than others in Sugar Valley.

A specific incident involving Prince and Ethel occurred on a hot summer day. Ethel, wearing gumboots, (high rubber footwear) was working with her dad in the fields when Prince arrived. Ethel's daughter, Beulah, relates how "Prince said something to her about the fact that her Pap was so cheap that he wouldn't buy her a decent pair of shoes; but made her run in hot gumboots in the middle of the summer, and that Pap 'takes care of the horses' feet better than he does yours'". Her daughter tells how young Ethel "took it as a sort-of joke; but, several days later, she had a new pair of shoes. She never knew where they came from – whether Pap was embarrassed or what – but she got a new pair of shoes!"

Not surprisingly, Prince Farrington was a frequent visitor with Floyd Klobe. Floyd, too, combined experience with skill to create another income to supplement his farm earnings. His friendship with Farrington was obviously one of mutual regard. It isn't known, today, whether there was a financial interest behind their friendship. As a young man, Floyd Klobe also worked as a moonshiner in New York City, a job discussed in Chapter Six.

Storing moonshine was another story, entirely, for Floyd Klobe. When he got company he'd grab a gun, as though he might be doing a little small-game hunting. With his gun, he'd walk to a stone pile in the middle of a field. There he apparently had a hidden stash of liquor. He'd retrieve a bottle of whiskey and return to his guests. Family members were sure that Floyd Klobe had a second hiding place beneath a massive straw pile behind the barn, a place forbidden to children.

Ethel Klobe's marriage to Earl Quiggle involved another irony. Ethel's moonshiner father, Floyd, used liquor; but was not an alcoholic. Her husband was. She and her toper spouse were the parents of three children, including Beulah Quiggle Neff, who now lives in Howard, Pennsylvania where she helps preserve the history of one of Sugar Valley's most colorful families. As explained in Chapter Six, Beulah is also the individual responsible for the preservation of two stills that once belonged to the Klobe clan.

Prince Farrington clung to his moonshining ways until his health and legal woes forced him to quit. Floyd Curtis Klobe, on the other hand, stopped making moonshine while a young man. It happened, the family believes, when he and his teen-aged daughter, Ethel, were cooking a fresh batch in the still beneath the shed. She had been taught the process. The father and daughter were surprised to see some revenue agents entering the farm lane. Floyd left Ethel to cap the still while he hurried to meet the revenuers. While Floyd kept the revenuers occupied, his teen-aged daughter worked to cap the still, so that it would stop cooking. The still might have exploded. Floyd recognized the danger. He later confessed, "I might have killed my daughter!" The family thinks that that was the last moonshine that Floyd ever made.

STALKED BY TRAGEDY

Beulah Quiggle Neff has observed, "I know that my grandfather (Floyd Klobe) did illegal things; but he was a good person. He was very, very good to us. Unfortunately, Floyd Curtis Klobe expressed a fear that he was to become a victim of senseless tragedy. He had solid reasons. His grandfather had been murdered in

Philadelphia. Then his father, Herman Klobe, was killed during the brawl between Floyd Klobe and Louis B. Huntingdon. His fear was palpably reinforced when he was sitting on a bar stool in a tavern near Jersey Shore. A man suddenly came from behind and stabbed Floyd in the back!" The attack was nearly successful; Floyd was severely injured; but he survived. However, his fear of being murdered was reinforced and he was convinced that the stabbing had been done under orders from a man in Lock Haven. There was also the 1929 automobile accident that took the life of his ex-wife, Thressa. Despite his fears, Floyd Curtis Klobe actually died a natural death. Sadly, there was one more senseless killing of a family member that Floyd would know before his own passing.

Forty-year-old Leo Held lived in Loganton and worked at the Hammermill Paper Company plant in Lock Haven. At one time or another, he had been a volunteer fireman, school board director and scout leader. On the morning of October 23, 1967, Leo Held went on a rampage, seemingly resulting from annoyances and grievances magnified. He strode into the Hammermill plant armed with a 45-calibre automatic pistol and a 38-calibre magnum revolver. There he shot and killed five of his superiors. He also wounded four others. Then he went to the nearby Piper Aircraft factory and shot and injured a woman who was a member of his carpool. Carpool members were said to have criticized Held's reckless driving. He then returned, via a back road, to his hometown, Loganton.

In Loganton, he drove around the school where three of his children were in attendance. He saw no one outside and drove away. The tale of terror had preceded him. The children were all locked within the school. The man who lived across the street from Leo Held, was a 28-year-old man named Quiggle. Held had complained to Quiggle about smoke from Quiggle's burning leaves. Quiggle also had a collection of guns. On that fateful day, his wife, Donna, had already taken their son to school and returned. One relative told of Held bursting into the Quiggle home and rushing upstairs to where Quiggle was still in bed. When his wife saw Held, she grabbed the telephone and shoved her daughter under the bed. Leo Held shot the phone out of her hand. As Quiggle started to rise, Held shot and killed him. As Donna Quiggle leaned over her husband, Held shot her in the back. She survived for another ten years, but spent that decade as a paralyzed cripple. With the terrified Quiggle child left unshot, Held hurried downstairs and smashed the locked door of Quiggle's gun cabinet. He wrapped an armful of rifles in some bedding and returned to his own house. Held sat weapons at each window, in an apparent plan to face authorities from his own barricaded house. Held next emerged from his house, intent on killing an elderly woman who lived in a nearby mobile home. He never got to the mobile home. As lawmen closed in, Held was defiant, shouting: "Come and get me. I'm not taking any more of their bull!" Held's lawn was the scene of the firefight. Despite the pleading of a brother-in-law, and having been hit by several officers' bullets, Held continued to return fire until he collapsed from his multiple wounds. He died in the hospital, a couple of days later, without ever fully regaining consciousness.

Four observations regarding the 1967 Leo Held rampage in Clinton County:

- The local people showed the same concern for Leo Held's family members as they did for the family members of his shooting victims.
- It was the worst such shooting spree in Clinton County history.
- The killing spree occurred less than 15 months after the Texas Tower shooting rampage of Charles Whitman; a killing spree that left 16 people dead and 32 others wounded at the University of Texas in Austin.
- The innocent 28-year-old man from Loganton, who was senselessly shot to death because his leaf-burning smoke drifted, or because he had some coveted guns, was Floyd Quiggle, son of Ethel Klobe Quiggle and grandson of the man for whom he was named, Floyd Klobe. The Quiggles had also named *their* son – the one who was safely in school – for their ancestor, Floyd Curtis Klobe.

Floyd Curtis Klobe, who had been born 85 years earlier at Carroll, died January 12, 1979. Floyd's daughter, Ethel Klobe Quiggle, died March 24, 1991. Etta Raudabaugh, the widow who lived with Floyd Klobe for the last half century of his life – and who was recognized as 'mother' by Thressa Klobe's daughter, Ethel – outlived her unofficial stepdaughter, dying November 30, 1991. All three, Floyd, Etta and Ethel rest, side-by-side in the Fairview Cemetery at Loganton, where Ethel shares a grave and a headstone with her husband, Earl Quiggle. The tombstone of Ethel and Earl is decorated with two sketches: Earl's Mack truck and Ethel, in hunting garb and holding a rifle, eyeing a handsome buck deer.

An inexplicable oddity was revealed with Floyd Klobe's death: In his will, he had bypassed both his common-law wife of a half-century, Etta, and his lone child, Ethel. Etta's life-long contribution to the family finances was forgotten. Both women were saddened. Floyd's heirs were his three grandchildren! His legal heirs, however, agreed to re-divide the Floyd Klobe estate to give both Etta and Ethel their proper shares. Beulah Quiggle Neff remains philosophical about the turn of events. She jokes, "Why didn't Floyd Klobe start a *legal* distillery? Then, we wouldn't be worried about money."

Today most, including Steve Neff, think of their families' past not as being shameful; but as being colorful. So it was.

The gravestone of Zenadah "Nade" Farrington Coltrane, 1896-1934, beloved sister of Prince Farrington.

WHITEY'S CARS

WHOLESALE OUTLET NO. 1

NEW and USED CARS

601 W. CHURCH ST.   ORLANDO, FLA.

The business card of Prince David Farrington, Jr. ("Whitey") for his new/used car business, one of his several enterprises.

An old photograph showing a Civilian Conservation Corps (CCC) camp near Renovo, Clinton County, PA. Courtesy of former CCC member, Leonard Parucha.

Bunny Wright and her brother, Tony Hyatt, flanking the Farrington stone inthe Burnett's Chapel graveyard, near Greensboro, North Carolina.

A Klobe family relic. A still that once steamed near Carroll as property of Floyd Klobe.

The tombstone for Ethel Klobe Quiggle and her husband, Earl, whose Mack truck appears, opposite Ethel's depiction as a huntress. Mountain View Cemetery in Loganton, Clinton County, PA.

The home of Gladys and George Porter and their family, near Torbert, Lycoming County. Prince Farrington was said to have had a still in the basement here at one time.

Juxtaposed: Trucks used in the Marcellus shale gas extraction process, loading water from the Susquehanna River. In the background, on the top of the cliff is the mansion of the late Prince David Farrington.

A 'recipe' book for making a variety of alcoholic concoctions. Apparently printed in Philadelphia and once owned by one or more of the Klobe family members. A Klobe family heirloom.

A bottle-capping device that was once owned by Prince Farrington; but is now one of the moonshining collectibles at the Gamble Farm Inn in Jersey Shore.

A metal panel that once marked an upstairs apartment as being named for Prince Farrington. Second floor doorway at the Gamble Farm Inn.

Three moonshiners at an unknown location. Note the complexity of the operation, with the wooden containers, the still, a lean-to, a couple of tents and a large number of kegs and barrels. This print was once owned by the late Joe Gardner, who had it hanging in his living room Lock Haven.

FARRINGTON GREAT RACE REVIVAL

ylvania's Premier Run, Canoe, Bike Triathlon
Saturday, July 26, 2003
Williamsport, PA

mile bicycle course begins at Indian Park
: - 4 mile canoe course begins and ends at the Greevy Boat Launch
RUN - 5K (3.1 miles) run begins at Greevy Boat Launch and ends at Indian Park

t-shirt for each participant. Entry fee of $20 per team member due by July 19, 2003, to American Red Cross, port, PA 17701. Late fee of $10 per team for entries received after July 19, 2003. Male age group determined of July 26, 2003. Bicyclists must obey all race rules and traffic laws or face disqualification. No track bikes

Self-explanatory poster. Several decades after Prince Farrington died, he name graced the posters of a fund-raising event. This event was held for ten or eleven years before interest waned.

RES. OF M. A. GAMBLE,
JERSEY SHORE, LYCOMING CO., PA

A 19th century drawing of the Gamble Farm, on the edge of what is now Jersey Shore. The house was converted into an inn many decades later. Courtesy of Wayne Welshans.

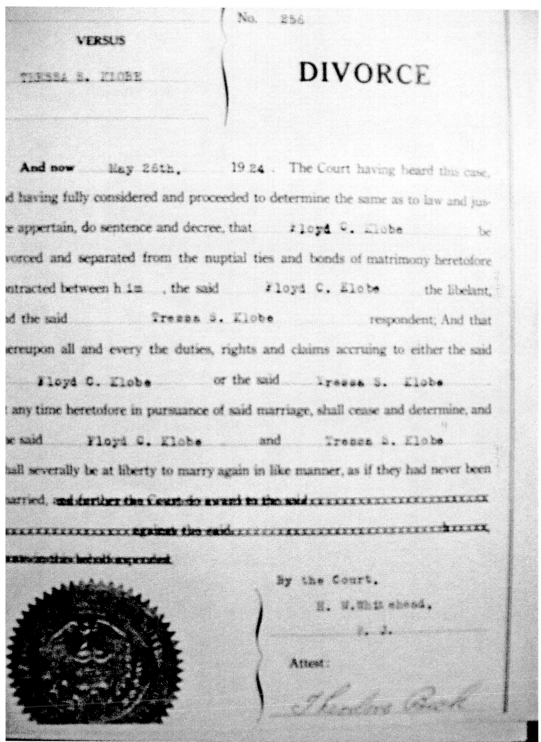

No. 256

VERSUS

TRESSA S. KLOBE

DIVORCE

And now May 26th, 19 24. The Court having heard this case, and having fully considered and proceeded to determine the same as to law and justice appertain, do sentence and decree, that Floyd C. Klobe be divorced and separated from the nuptial ties and bonds of matrimony heretofore contracted between h im , the said Floyd C. Klobe the libelant, and the said Tressa S. Klobe respondent; And that thereupon all and every the duties, rights and claims accruing to either the said Floyd C. Klobe or the said Tressa S. Klobe at any time heretofore in pursuance of said marriage, shall cease and determine, and the said Floyd C. Klobe and Tressa S. Klobe shall severally be at liberty to marry again in like manner, as if they had never been married, and further the Court do award to the said xxxxxxxxxxxxxxxxxxxxxxx xxxxxxxxxxxxxxxxx against the said xxxxxxxxxxxxxxxxxxxxxxxxxxxxxxxxxx xxxxxxxxxx hereinbefore expressed.

By the Court,

H. W.Whitehead,

P. J.

Attest:

Theodore Beck

The Lycoming County divorce decree that ended the marriage of Tressa (Thressa) Klobe and Floyd Klobe.

Keg hoops found at a Prince Farrington still site on the lands that were once part of the Florida Fruit Farm. Photo by the author.

A helicopter involved in the geological survey of Clinton County as part of the Marcellus shale gas boom. When not surveying the area's geological features deep beneath the surrounding hills, it rests near the Restless Oaks restaurant at McElhattan.

The Rauchtown Inn, in the heart of Farrington country, between Antes Fort and Carroll. The road on the left leads to Carroll and to the exit of Interstate 80.

Three of Prince Farrington's workers, relaxing on steps of his old house at the Florida Fruit Farm.

Depicted here are four friends of Prince Farrington: From left: DeWitt ("Pud") Hill, Lemuel Groce, Charles ("Charl") Farrington and Colonel Segraves.

Treasurers of local lore, John Wagner, Dave Frankenberger and Harold "Dutch" Washburn at the Twilight Diner, just outside of Loganton.   All are Sugar Valley residents.

James Segraves III, by a woodland stream just off Jack's Hollow Road, near the town of Bastress. The stream and the fog-shrouded path both lead to a long-abandoned still site once used by James' great grandfather, the moonshiner friend of Prince Farrington, Colonel Monte Segraves.

A ceramic tile silo on the farm once occupied by Prince Farrington's friend, DeWitt Hill and located just south of Jersey Shore, Lycoming County.

The grand entrance to the Victoria Theater in Jersey Shore, PA., where the young Farringtons and their friends saw the current fare out of the Hollywood movie studios. Courtesy of Wayne Welshans.

Thressa Klobe's grave stone, near Loganton.

Prince Farrington (right), with his close associate, Joe Gardner, and Joe's son, Neese.

Thressa Klobe, one of the several unique women in Prince and the Paupers. A metropolitan chorus girl, an absentee mother, whose life was abruptly shortened by a tragic automobile accident.

83

A trio of Farrington workers burying or disinterring some illegal alcohol.

A pair of vintage autos; once prizes of the wealthy. The rear one belonged to Prince Farrington.

Colonel Monte Segraves, one of Prince Farrington's close friends, with his first wife, the former Marie Engel. He was from North Carolina; she from the Bastress area of Lycoming County.

Gladys Farrington Porter as a young woman.

Gladys Farrington Porter, Prince's lone daughter, with her first two offspring.

Early American family life is captured in this picture of Bernard Wynn's grandmother, Maggie Duck Bower, his aunt Ruth and the family cow, on their homestead on Rockey Road, near Loganton.

Prince Farrington, Jr. "Whitey" on a family tractor.

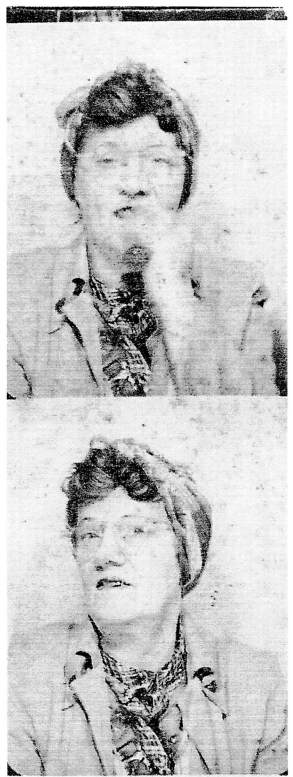

*The moonshiner's troubled wife, Martha
(Mrs. Prince) White Farrington.*

Prince Farrington's friend, Joe Gardner, telling two of his nephews about the grand still he remembered working near Greensboro, North Carolina.

Boyd "Duke" Greak, with his children, Barbara (now Clark) and Lee.

B. W. Coltrane, a popular member of the Farrington relation, in military attire.

B. W. Coltrane with a native during B. W.'s overseas service.

Mr. and Mrs. Boyd "Duke" Greak. He successfully transformed from a Farrington worker to a married man who loved hunting, fishing, and nature in general.

The gravestone of Margaret and Herman Klobe, in Eastville.

Prince Farrington, Jr. ("Whitey") and his uncle, Scott Anthony, who was married to his mother's sister.

A memorial brick, near Newport, Virginia, placed in Prince Farrington's memory by his grandson, Dr. Robert Porter.

Two of Charl Farrington's children, Frances (later Mrs. George Gardner) and her brother, Robert.

A long-time friend of Prince Farrington, Earl W. "Skinny" Ritter, proud of his '29 Nash.

GIRTY'S FACE ON THE
SUSQUEHANNA TRAIL
PA. - 159

"Girty's Notch," a landmark along Routes 11 and 15 north of Harrisburg, said to represent the colonial renegade, Simon Girty.

Etta Place & the Sundance Kid.
~ New York 1901~

De Young Studios. Broadway. New York

Popular portrait of Pennsylvania-born western outlaw, Harry Longabaugh ("The Sundance Kid") and his mistress, Etta Place.

A monument to the man from Mont Clare, Pennsylvania, Harry Longabaugh, erected in Sundance, Wyoming.

An early seasonal greeting card from Prince Farrington to his family.

A common portrait of Prince Farrington in his more mature years.

Pine Creek Hollow.
Feb. the 9th/88

Dearest and best
yours of the 5th instant
at hand, I feel very lonesome
since you have left, time
seems long to me, for instance
when Saturday night comes
I had bin out on Wednesday.
evening But you had gone
of so I felt disstointed.

A 19th century love letter, self-adorned by the artistic swain, Herman Henry Klobe.

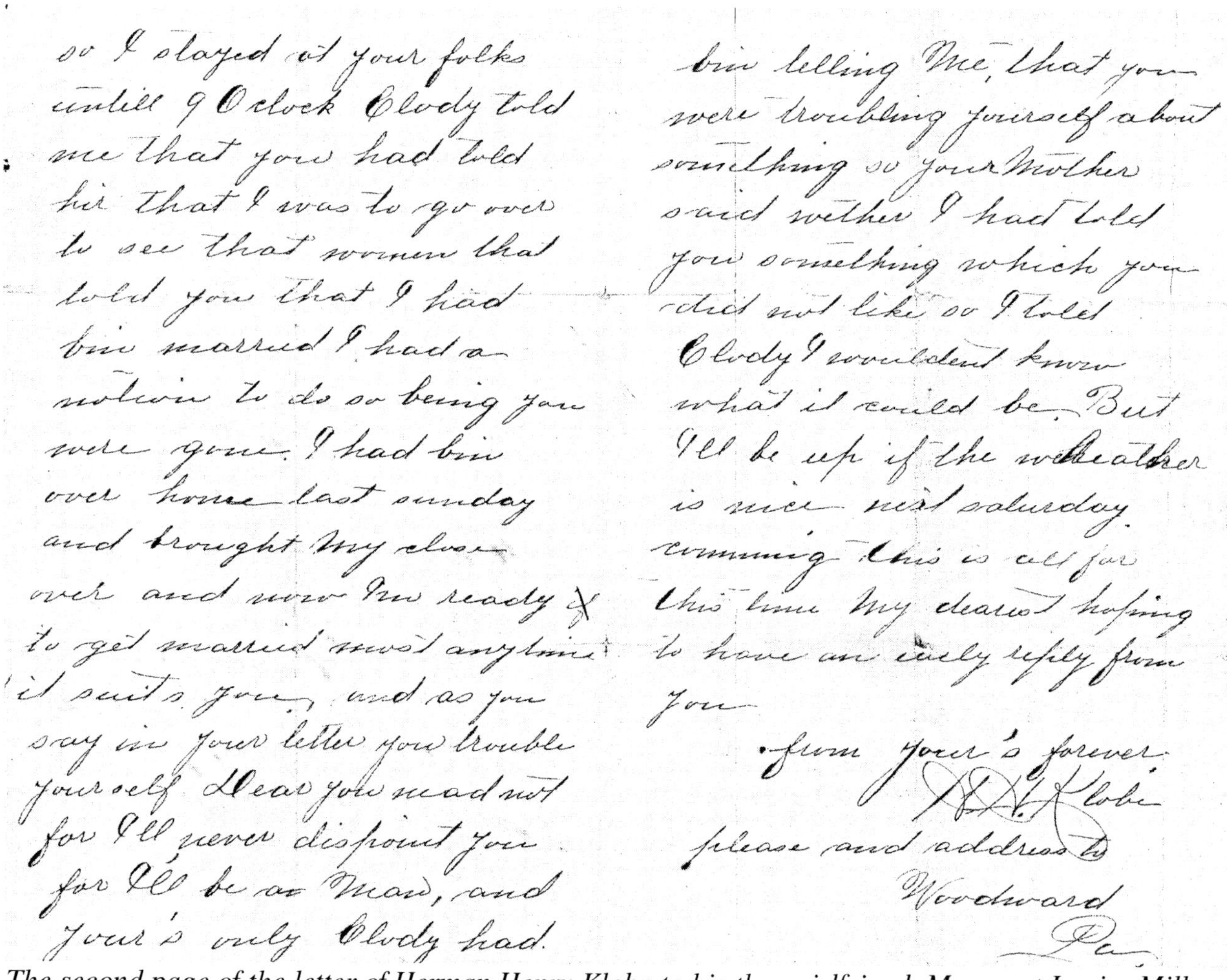

so I stayed at your folks untill 9 Oclock Clody told me that you had told her that I was to go over to see that women that told you that I had bin married I had a notion to do so being you were gone. I had bin over home last sunday and brought my close over and now Im ready to get married most anytime it suits you, and as you say in your letter you trouble yourself Dear you mad not for I'll never dispoint you for I'll be a man, and Your's only Clody had.

bin telling me, that you were troubling yourself about something so your Mother said wither I had told you something which you did not like so I told Clody I wouldent know what it could be. But I'll be up if the weather is nice next saturday comming this is all for this time My dearest hoping to have an early reply from you

from Your's forever
H. H. Klobe
please and address to
Woodward
Pa

The second page of the letter of Herman Henry Klobe to his then girlfriend, Margaret Louise Miller.

106

LEO TAYLOR   "Chippy"
Athletic Club 2, 3, 4; Science Nature
Club 3, 4; Athletic Association 2; Foot-
ball 2, 3, 4; Basketball 1.

Special! Gridiron hero remorseful!

"Chippy" is quite remorseful these days
simply because of graduation. And you
know what that will mean — his days
on the gridiron will be no more. "Chippy" has been one swell member of our
A-1 football gang. Wonder if Miss Edith
thinks the same as we do!

GEORGE PORTER   "Greg"
Alumni Treasurer of Class 3; Band 1,
2, 3, 4; Custodian 4; Journalism Club 3,
4; Concert Orchestra 3; Dance Orchestra
2, 3; *Orange and Black* Staff 4.

Extra! Buster busts buttons!

"Little Buster Porter,
Had lost his quarter,
So he looked in his mit,
But upon it he did sit!"
Ahem! That will be the day.

GLADYS FARRINGTON   "Foxey"

Science Nature 2, Secretary 2; Athletic
Association 1, 2, 3, 4; Sigma Delta Chi
4; Student Council 3, 4; Alumni Treasurer 2; Secretary of Class 3; Class Play 4.

*"Fair to look upon but better yet to
know."*

Three yearbook entries from the appropriate Jersey Shore High School yearbooks.

*An authentic Prince Farrington specimen,
now owned by Kim VanCampen, whose
father received it as a gift.*

The McElhattan (Clinton County) home of author/fabulist Colonel Henry W. Shoemaker.

The old paint mill on Antes Creek, said to have been used for hiding Farrington moonshine.

Bernie Wynn leaning against his dad's 1929 Dodge. Taken at the Bower homestead, on Rockey Road, about three miles from the Florida Fruit Farm of Prince Farrington.

CHAPTER SIX

A Roadshow of Relics

THE HOME ON SILVER AVENUE

Those who appreciate local lore must be especially grateful to those owners of history-rich houses or estates who dedicate the time and finances to the restoration of their properties. This was mentioned in *Prohibition's Prince* (I: 136-7; 151-6), regarding the Stewart-Courtright property that sits along the Susquehanna River near Antes Fort. That majestic home was once the centerpiece of a 19th century estate, where it served as a farmhouse and a refuge for runaway slaves. Under the ownership of Prince Farrington, the building shared family quarters with distilling equipment and, at one time, a speakeasy. That historic homestead is now being restored to an earlier majesty by its present owners, Pat and Phil Courtright.

Similarly, a magnificent property sits on Silver Avenue in the village of Lamar, near the interchange of mile 173 on Interstate 80. This stately three-story home was built in 1895 by James A. Wolfenden, a native of England. Wolfenden was an engineer who was employed in Pittsburgh. He hobnobbed with Henry Ford and contributed to the design of Ford's first automobile. Wolfenden also flew the American Flag; although on one day each year, the queen's birthday, he flew the British "Union Jack." Several decades after its construction, the grand home on Silver Avenue was considered as a possible Pennsylvania governors' mansion. Wolfenden pushed that proposal; but his political influence couldn't outweigh the distance from Harrisburg. When Prince Farrington lived near Loganton, he lived about 12 miles due east of Lamar. When Prince wanted his brother, Charles's, support in his moonshining/bootlegging enterprises, the house was a convincing part of the package. The home's four previous owners couldn't have envisioned the wildly new role that the house would play.

Charles (Charl) and his wife, Virginia (Virgie) lived in the three-story home for the remainder of their lives. The Silver Avenue mansion saw distilling in the basement and beneath the foundation of the nearby chicken house. It saw Charles and his brother, Prince Farrington, sitting on the back stoop and downing whiskey together. It saw black-suited agents raiding and moving through the house like ants through a cupboard. It saw arrests of its patriarch as well as its matriarch. It saw children, grandchildren and other relatives and friends celebrating life with music and moonshine. Then, within one year, 1971, it saw the passing of Virgie and Charl and the passing of the colorful role it had experienced for several decades. Silver Avenue returned to its former tree-shaded solitude.

The fact that the home was part of Prince and Charl Farrington's life, made everyone suspect that the mansion had hidden passages or false storage spaces for concealing booze. There were small closets; but they didn't conceal anything. The Victorian house on Silver Avenue was without any mysterious spaces. Even after the present owners, Nell and Tom Muir, moved into the property, no such hiding place was found. The Muirs did see a suspicious area in their house. Beneath one first-floor stairwell, was a closed space; but neither the steps, nor the wall opposite the steps, showed any way whatever to access the space beneath the stairs. However, after several years, the Muirs had some work done in the basement. The contractor noticed a small latch among the beams of the ceiling of the cellar. There it was! Unnoticed by everyone before, the contractor had found a well-disguised trapdoor that opened into the *bottom* of the space beneath the first-floor stairs. There, undiscovered for many years, was an authentic, secret storage area.

The bustling nature of Charl Farrington's Silver Avenue home was related before (I: 104-112). However, one gentleman who was a teen in Charl's heyday, Walter Overdorf, experienced his own Lamar episode. It was about 1943, just a year or two before Walt entered military service. It seems that Walt was sitting on the front steps of Cora Overdorf, his grandmother's house. This was in Booneville, in Sugar Valley, on a late Saturday afternoon. Bill Schrack and his cousin, Glenn Smith, drove up, stopped and asked Walt if he wanted to go along. He did. They didn't tell him of any particular destination. Glenn Bierly happened to be walking along the road at Booneville, so they stopped and picked up Bierly, too. Walt still had no idea where they were going; but it was Saturday evening in rural Clinton County and he was riding with friends. That was all one needed to know.

The four teens drove west through Tylersville, out of Sugar Valley and into the Fishing Creek Narrows. Just beyond the "Narrows" they entered the town of Lamar. The driver knew his destination. They were going down Silver Avenue to a Saturday night gathering at Charl Farrington's place. When they arrived, there were cars parked "all around the place."

As they walked onto the porch, Walt could see a huge juke box sitting inside and "blaring loudly." Suddenly, as Walt and his friends were trying to enter the house, everyone inside began shoving and pushing to get out! Police were rushing to join the party through the back door! Some escaping carouser grabbed Walt by the pants seat and his neck and tossed him over the porch bannister and into the bushes. Walt hid there momentarily before he and his three companions were able to leave without being stopped. That was Walt Overdorf's first, and last, visit to the house on Silver Avenue.

Several years later, after Walt was out of the military service, he and Nelson Wolfe were riding Wolfe's new, large, black 74 Harley-Davidson motorcycle, with overhead valves. The cycle was supposed to be able to reach a speed of 120 mph; but Walt says he only ever saw it hovering around 110 when he peeked over Wolfe's shoulder! They stopped at the Nittany Inn, near Lamar. There was only a bartender and one other patron. They asked for drinks; but the bartender refused. When they asked again, the lone customer growled, "Give the boys a goddam drink!" So they were served. Their patron? A customer who was so faithful that he had his own bottle opener at the Nittany Inn: Charl Farrington.

ANOTHER FLASK

Distinguished. That is the most appropriate word for one whose life had accomplishments piled one upon another. If you want to be convinced that the word is properly used here, look at the record of a Lycoming County native and lifelong resident, Dean R. Fisher (1924-2000). Fisher graduated from Jersey Shore High School and was in college when World War II erupted. He abandoned his studies in order to enlist in the U.S. Navy. He left service as an Ensign and later resigned his commission with the rank of Lieutenant, j.g. Fisher returned to school, enrolling at Muhlenberg College. He then got a law degree from the University of Pennsylvania. He was associated with many area fraternal and professional organizations for the coming decades, always demonstrating leadership and innovative skills. Dean R. Fisher's intellect, energy and humanity were shared with his wife and two children as well as the community.

One of Dean Fisher's public roles was as a member of the Pennsylvania Liquor Control Board. It was in that position that he received a gift of one of the few surviving bottles of Prince Farrington liquor. That relic was passed to his daughter, Kim, who provided pictures of that rare bottle of Farrington moonshine, for this biography of the king of moonshiners. A close look at the label indicates that one is reading the confiscation data for a bottle taken in 1948. The label also indicates that the bottle contains one pint of "moonshine" and it bears the name of Prince Farrington, apparently written on the label by a policing agent. Another bit of data: his flask is now a prized memento of Fisher's daughter, Kim VanCampen of Williamsport.

MEMORABLE GLASSES

In the early 1940s, Prince urged Earl Ritter to buy the Brown's Run flats, a property that was priced at $2,000. This land, coveted by Prince Farrington if someone else held title to it, was located in the remote Pine Creek valley, just south of Jersey Mills and close to where Route 44 and Route 414 split. Why would the moonshiner encourage a friend to buy this somewhat isolated real estate? Because Prince already had a still operating there and, if the property was owned by someone other than Prince, himself, it might avoid government scrutiny. However, Earl Ritter made an independent decision, since he wanted to own a different property, a farm owned by the Campbell brothers. The farm that Ritter actually acquired was located in the same general area, between Jersey Mills and Cammal. Also, although the farm had 546 acres, the asking price was a more modest $750.00. The still identified here by David Ritter will be more precisely pinpointed in Chapter Seven.

While still a pre-teen, David Ritter would accompany his father on visits to the *Gamble Farm Inn* or *Antiques Inn*. This was while Prince Farrington was staying there. Later, David Ritter graduated in the same Jersey Shore high school class as Prince's grandson, Craig Porter. Shortly after their graduation, Craig was killed in an auto accident (I: 201). Ritter notes that Gladys tried to restore an antique atmosphere at the Inn; but, he observes, as time passed things got broken or stolen. Gladys, who remembered the friendship of Earl Ritter and her dad, called Earl's son, David, and asked him to visit. That's when she gave him some of the remaining glasses used at the inn; the very glasses that once held drinks that were consumed in friendship by Earl and Prince.

EARL'S PRIDE AND JOY

Another relic worth showing is the 1929 Nash that belonged to Earl W. "Skinny" Ritter, another close friend of Prince Farrington. Ritter, mentioned in the previous article, eventually spent about four decades working for the *Pennsylvania Power and Light Company.* Ritter was a foreman at the *P.P. & L.* Jersey Shore substation and had supervisory duties over an area from the eastern edge of Lock Haven southeast to the area around Oriole. Ritter also declared that his '29 Nash automobile was the first car, *ever*, to climb up and over the Elimsport mountain in high gear!

A GENTLEMAN'S WALKING STICK.

The ancient Greeks had a riddle. What walks on four legs, then on two legs and, finally, on three legs? The nice thing about ancient riddles: Countless individuals have learned the answer. Who is unaware of the answer to this one? The answer is: *a human.* He, or she, crawls on all four limbs during infancy; walks upright and on two legs throughout childhood and most of adulthood; and finally, with debilitating age, walks with the support of a cane. At some point in his life, Prince Farrington carried a man's walking stick. The *walking stick* of the time was *not* meant to support the weight of an invalid; but was a fancy, *straight* stick to be used as part of a dapper wardrobe. This would have been before his worsening gangrene and the loss of several toes would have made a more substantial support vital to Prince's painful mobility. Also, among Farrington's several chauffeurs was one named Leroy Ruch of Duboistown. Ruch, was the eventual recipient of a gift from Prince: a walking stick. Ruch later worked until his retirement, for the *Pennsylvania Power and Light Company.* For years, Leroy Ruch and his wife, Mae, were close friends of another area couple, Dorothy and Howard Thomas. Ruch later gave the walking stick to Howard. Recently, Howard's widow, the lively-96-year old Dorothy Thomas, donated Prince Farrington's fancy walking stick to a local institution. Thus, through a nonagenarian's generosity, the walking stick that was once Prince Farrington's, is now a part of the museum treasures of the *Thomas T. Tabor Museum* in Williamsport, Pennsylvania.

A RESET GEM AND AN EMPTY RING

As a young man, Floyd Klobe, the moonshiner from rural Greene Township in Clinton County, Pennsylvania, worked for a New York City jeweler. A token of the jeweler's appreciation was the gift of a man's diamond ring, with a sizable stone. That 1927 night that Floyd Klobe was fighting with Louis Huntingdon, Klobe wore the ring. The condition of Huntingdon's face suggested that Klobe had made serious contact several times. He never wore the ring after that fateful night.

After Floyd's death, his daughter, Ethel, had the stone removed and reset into another diamond ring, resting between two smaller stones. This Ethel had done for herself. After her own death, both the diamond ring and the gem-less original became prized possessions of Floyd's granddaughter, Beulah.

KEG HOOPS FROM A FARRINGTON STILL SITE

Likely the most common Prince Farrington artifact that one might find today is the metal hoop from the long-abandoned barrels or kegs. About the year 2001, the author was introduced to one of the many Farrington still sites by Yvonne and Steve Weaver of Loganton. The site is on the *Florida Fruit Farm*, and was visited by leaving the rural road on the farm and following a small stream upwards, through a wooded slope. There, at the rivulet's source, was a small collecting pond, apparently constructed in Prince's early years in Pennsylvania, to create a more reliable water supply. One could see, nearby, some broken bricks, hoops and other detritus from a nearly century-old still. The author retrieved a pair of small rusting hoops, of 10 ½ and 12 ½ -inches diameter, the continued ownership of which was cleared through the courtesy of Bud Webb, the present owner of the legendary farm.

A BOTTLE CAPPING DEVICE

As mentioned in Chapter Eight, the Gamble Farm Inn, in Jersey Shore, possesses an authentic bottle-capping device once owned by Prince Farringon.

KLOBE'S RECIPE BOOKLET

There is a small booklet that is a mere twenty pages (ten folded sheets) and that measures about 3 1/2" by 6". A granddaughter absolutely identifies it as having belonged to Floyd Klobe. It was valuable enough to some in the Klobe family that it was passed through several generations and, when it began to fall apart, some concerned member of the family took what appears to have been black upholstery thread and crudely, but effectively, sewed the pages together. This booklet is a machine-printed document, filled with the recipes needed to create many types of liquor. The front cover is plain and sports a title, all in caps: HOW TO MAKE IT. Also on the cover, in smaller letters but still upper case: CANADIAN PUBLISHING CO. Adding to the mystery are the words of the very bottom two lines. They say: Office 2356 Washington Ave., Philadelphia Penna. The four-digit street number is not quite clear; and is assumed to be the number given.

Why was the Canadian Publishing Co. publishing a booklet in Philadelphia? We have no answer. One guess is that this was printed either just before Prohibition or shortly thereafter, since it openly identifies itself and its address. However, this may not be true. The entire cover could have been a fraud. All we know, with certainty, is that the interior pages are crammed with some precautionary advice for using the recipes and with the recipes themselves. The list, with original spellings: Whiskey Egg Nogg; Wine Lemonade; Auto Cocktail; Bourbon; Corn Whiskey; Scotch; Cognac Brandy; Raisin Brandy; Slivovitz (a prune and brown sugar concoction); Rye Whiskey with Malt Flavor; Malt Whiskey from Ground Malt; Malt Whiskey from Whole Barley Malt; Home Made Lager; Wild Cherry Wine; Elderberry Wine; Raisin Wine; Plain Alcohol; Dandelion Wine; Kimmel; Whole Rye Whiskey; Whiskey from Ground Rye; Sprouted Rye Whiskey; Fruit Mashes; Apricot Brandy; Apple Jack; Red Beet Wine; California Port Wine from Grape Juice; Apricot Wine; Dream (lemon juice with gin flavor, etc.); Brandy Julep; Elks' Delight; Grape Wine; Blackberry and Huckleberry Wine; Blackberry Cordial; Gin; Gordon Gin; Rum; Beauty Cocktail; Beauty Spot Cocktail and Bird Cocktail. The back cover helpfully explains how one can convert many of these recipes into barrel lots. At the right time and the right place, such a booklet could have given someone a lucrative vocation.

One drink listed in that old booklet was a puzzler. What is *kimmel*? Dictionaries were consulted, including *The Oxford Universal Dictionary* – a word authority that lists hundreds of obsolete words. Internet searches were similarly fruitless. Finally, some sleuthing by staff members of the Bloomsburg (PA) Field Office of the Penn State Extension program yielded an answer: *Kimmel* is a Yiddish term, based on a German word. It indicates that the drink had a caraway source.

THE MILLHEIM STEAM BOILER

Two of the Klobe stills, a large one and a miniature model, remain as treasured family relics. The larger of the two has been moved twice since Floyd Klobe's death. That still was once used by the Klobe family patriarch, Herman, and his son, Floyd. While it was still making moonshine for him, Floyd moved the still from place to place near his Sugar Valley home. When Floyd Klobe died, his granddaughter, Beulah Quiggle Neff (widow of the late Robert Neff) and her son, Steve Neff, removed the still from its last Sugar Valley hiding place, beneath the floor of a shed. Beulah and Steve loaded the copper boiler and its several attachments onto the back of an old Ford pickup truck and took it to the Neff property in the town of Howard (Centre County). Since Beulah was always nervous about having the still nearby and fearful that the years might not stop revenuers from appearing, the still was kept hidden, even in Howard. Today, Steve, great grandson and great-great grandson of moonshiners, operates a funeral home in Howard and in Millheim and he has moved the still to a garage near his business in Millheim (also Centre County). Today, the many descendants of the moonshiners/bootleggers of Clinton and Lycoming counties can enjoy discussing the ghosts that still linger in their family closets. We all benefit from their willingness to share that colorful past.

§ § §

CHAPTER SEVEN

And Yet, More Stills

If one began following a stream in Sugar Valley, during the days of Prohibition, what were the odds of locating an illegal whiskey distilling operation? There are no statistics, of course; but the late Dan Schrack once observed (personal conversation, 6/10/04) that, "It seems that where almost all the streams in the area ended, there was a still." Readers of the earlier book (I: Chapter 8) may recall that the sites of over 30 stills were identified, all of which were believed to have been operated, at one time or another, by Prince Farrington. We now know that one of those sites, the one that disappeared beneath the Lock Haven reservoir, was owned by John Wagner's father, Walt. We can now add the precise locations of another dozen sites; but without certainty regarding which were or were not those of Prince Farrington.

1. Beneath the Shed on Winter Road

A couple of roads run from one end of Sugar Valley to the other. Sugar Valley folks refer to the two roads as the Winter Road and the Summer Road. Winter Road runs East-West along the lower ridges on the south side of the valley. On the opposite side of the valley, running roughly parallel with the Winter Road, is the Summer Road. There are about a half-dozen connecting roads that cross the valley, between the large farms and small villages. For some years, Floyd Curtis Klobe lived on a farm on the Winter Road. Hidden there, was one of several of Floyd's stills.

His granddaughter, Beulah Quiggle Neff, could say, "I know that Pap made whiskey at the farm. He dug the side out of the shed and made an underground basement. The still was under there. On the first floor, he had a trapdoor, as well as a workbench and so on. You know, it looked like a shop; but I don't think he was fooling anyone." However, authorities never found any of Floyd Klobe's stills. In the 1980s he sold the farm. He then built a shed attached to his daughter's shed. Although there was never any activity involved with that newer shed, it was padlocked and Floyd warned, "You don't ever get in there!" Shortly after Floyd died, his curious daughter and granddaughter left the door padlocked; but unscrewed the hinges and peeked inside. Somehow, unseen by the family, he had sneaked his old still into the shed. That is the one that later found a home in Howard.

2. Close by the Beaver Dam

Beulah Quiggle Neff, as a child spent considerable time with her Pap, Floyd Klobe.   Apparently Floyd was satisfied that Beulah accepted his law-breaking lifestyle. On one occasion, he allowed his daughter, Ethel, and his granddaughter, Beulah, to accompany him on a visit to a still site that is now forever lost beneath Interstate 80. Although Beulah didn't see any still at the site, he identified the area as one of his still sites. She did note the small stream that flowed into the area, apparently from a source in nearby Fourth Gap. This is the same still that was identified (I: 142) in *Prohibition's Prince*.

3. Somewhere Near McCall's Dam

There is a largely unpaved mountain road connecting the town of Eastville, in Sugar Valley, Clinton County, with Route 192 in Union County. A tiny park, McCall's Dam State Park sits roughly midway between the two ends of that road. The road is closed and impassable for several winter months. It may have had just the isolation needed for a clandestine operation. There, a family member reports, the Klobes were believed to have operated an illegal still.

4. The Still Near Tea Spring

Although one or both of the Klobe brothers had known still sites in Floyd Klobe's shed and another was located near a beaver dam, while a third was located beneath what is now the great causeway known as Interstate 80, a fourth Klobe still site was back in the mountains near a natural feature known as the Tea Spring. This is believed to be the same site where three Klobes – Charles, Sr., his wife and one of his sons – was arrested, as described in Chapter Five. That spring is still so labeled on topographic maps. That still site is also further identified in the opening paragraphs of Chapter Eight.

5/6. Pickett's Pair

Ed Pickett is a Sugar Valley resident and a retired military veteran. Several decades ago, Pickett and his sons fished the area's mountain streams. One site visited was down an old wagon road near Fourth Gap Road, southeast of Ravensburg State Park. There, in Wagner's Hollow, Pickett reports, he and his children would fish for 'brookies' (Brook Trout). They had the necessary grease and gear so that they could cook and eat their catch by the stream. They could easily identify areas where people had discarded garbage over the years; but they saw, as well, two clearly-discernible areas that had debris that was much more specialized. They saw barrel staves, broken glass and the hoops that came from whiskey kegs. The Picketts saw enough relics to identify two long-abandoned distilling sites. Their location suggests that they might have been important moonshining operations for either one of the Klobes or for Prince Farrington.

7. Where Brown's Run Gurgles Forth

This still site has been identified by Dave Ritter of Trout Run. The operation was located at the very upper end of Brown's Run, which would place it about seven miles west of the run's mouth on Pine Creek. However, it would be much more accessible if one were to drive north, on Route 44, from Haneyville and then walk a few hundred yards to the stream's source; but that route would only make sense to someone who knew what he sought.

8/9. Two, Through A Nimrod's Eyes

Warren Gottshall has told us, and given us an annotated topographic map, where two stills had once boiled and distilled near the village of Caldwell. Until the Marcellus shale oil outfits began prospecting in the area, Gottshall and the other residents of Coudersport Pike corridor knew the beauty of the phrase, "splendid isolation." The area was ideal for hunting game or hiding stills.

As a young man, Warren Gottshall had been shown the two nearby stills and their abandoned apparatus. According to his carefully annotated map, one of the stills was in an area known as "Whiskey Hollow," an area visited many times by Mr. Gottshall while hunting deer and bear. That still sat only about two miles from the farm where Gottshall grew up and where he lives today. He often saw the remnants – brick, crockery and rusted metal – of the moonshiner's trade. Gottshall saw the other site less often, while hunting ruffed grouse as a teen. Both sites, which sit about a mile apart, are north of Swissdale and within a mile west of Route 664. That places them slightly less than five miles and slightly more than five miles, respectively, northwest of the clothing manufacturing town of Woolrich, in Clinton County.

10. In the Spring Garden pump house

This one was the Farrington still, northwest of Allenwood that was identified in Chapter One.

11. Rote's Still in Ram Hollow

Ed Rote did some moonshining. His lone still was located at the head of Ram Hollow, near the village of Swissdale. The waters from Ram Hollow form a small stream that flows nearly due west and empties into the Susquehanna River a couple of miles downstream from Queens Run.

Leroy Wenker remembers a time when Rote saw several of the Wenker boys and remarked, "Oh, you Wenker boys! Your great uncle, C. Irvin Wenker, told me when revenuers were coming. He'd let me know and I'd give him a jug of whiskey." Rote also related an incident when revenue agents came to his place looking for moonshine whiskey. Rote went into his cellar and brought out a jug of cider. They accepted enough cider that Rote had to descend into his cellar again for another jug. Ed Rote bragged that the lawmen got drunk on cider and left without ever finding his whiskey.

Leroy Wenker's great uncle, C. Irvin Wenker, was in an excellent position to warn a friend when revenue agents were about to pounce. C. Irvin Wenker was the sheriff. Although Wenker might warn a moonshiner of an impending raid, there was a limit to his disregard for the law. When alcohol was confiscated and put away for trial, Sheriff Wenker was offered $1,000 if he would let the key lying where someone might just find it. Wenker refused.

12. About Three Miles from Antes Fort.

One must go to where the information is. Sam Fuller, Bob Johnson, Ed Carothers and Bob Miller are just a few of the local sages gathered at Ed and Gerrie Snook's

Thursday morning flea market crowd, in Antes Fort. All have knowledge that they willingly share. Bob Miller, for example, told of seeing an old still, of unknown ownership, about three miles south of Antes Fort off Route 44. That abandoned still remained in place until the mid-1950s, when the equipment was later sold as junk.

13. Incriminating Pipes Off Jack's Hollow Road

Getting along with one's spouse is important; but, sometimes it is also helpful to get along with the in-laws, particularly if one needs an isolated place to make a little moonshine. Several of Prince's stills were not listed in *Prohibition's Prince* and remained unknown to the author. Thanks to Carol and James Segraves, one more excellent site can now be identified.

It was here that James father, Colonel Segraves, had operated a still. He and several other men would arrive at Engels for breakfast for several days running. After breakfast they would disappear into the woods. One day, James half-sister, Teresa, decided to follow them. She learned what they were doing when they noticed her behind them and sent her away with a sharp rebuke, "Never come down here again. Don't tell *anyone* what you saw here!" What she had seen was a fully operational still, beside a spring with a pipe channeling the water. At the spring there were large pines, around which there was a large turn-around on which a horse-pulled wagon could maneuver easily.

A REFLECTION

The aging equipment and supplies, once critical parts of someone's moonshining operation, have been idle for decades. None can go there today and smell the distinctive aroma of grain cooking and pushing steam through the coils in order to feed droplets of pure whiskey into large containers. None can watch as the liquor is reworked in order to reduce the alcohol content for human consumption. Nor can they observe the casks and kegs holding liquor that is being aged for several years before bottling and shipping to the thirsty imbibers who lived close to the stills or who lived a thousand miles away. With a thirst to slake and their money in hand, they had helped Prince Farrington amass a fortune that flowed through his hands as if he was trying to hold the intoxicating liquid itself.

CHAPTER EIGHT

The Legend Expanding

THE KEYSTONE STATE RENEGADES' ROSTER

Pennsylvania has had its share of significant renegades. Among those worthy of mention would be the following half dozen, whose lives spanned the years from about 1741 until 1956. All six likely had ancestry in the British Isles, with the likelihood that all six were descended from Scotch or Irish or both. Further, the lives of two of those listed were the subjects of movies. Lastly, all six renegades from the Keystone State have, for better or for worse, enriched the commonwealth's history.

SIMON GIRTY (c. 1741 – 1818) ~ Sometimes known as "the white savage," Simon Girty has been both praised and damned by researchers. A child of the Pennsylvania frontier, Girty had a father and a step-father killed by Indians. Girty, himself, spent several youthful years living with the Seneca Indians before becoming an interpreter. During the American Revolution, Girty sided with the British and led several brutal Indian raids against colonial Americans. Contemporary accounts suggest that he was sometimes merciless and sometimes compassionate. Eventually, Girty, pensioned by the British, fled to Canada and lived on a farm near Fort Malden (now Amherstburg) in Ontario until he died in 1818. His notoriety was such that he was included in a noted, fictional American short story, Stephen Vincent Benet's "The Devil and Daniel Webster."

DAVID BRADFORD (1760 – c. 1808) ~ David Bradford was a lawyer in southwestern Pennsylvania when the young federal government put a tax on whiskey (1791). People of the region felt that the tax unfairly burdened the frontier distillers. Still, there was only mild reaction to the tax until serious efforts were made to collect it. Then (1794) there was such strong resistance to the tax that officials were tarred and feathered and one official's home was torched. The best-known leader of this "Whiskey Rebellion" was Bradford. President George Washington ordered troops to crush this rebellion; which quickly fizzled as soldiers approached.

David Bradford got aboard a coal barge and fled down the Ohio River. He took up residence in Louisiana, then a Spanish territory. Although President John Adams pardoned him in 1799, Bradford remained in Louisiana as a wealthy landowner, until his death in late 1807 or early 1808.

DAVID LEWIS (1788 – 1820) ~ As happens with many legendary individuals, the stories of David "Davey" Lewis are based on facts, legends and some willfully-perverted accounts.   Centre County historian, Douglas Macneal (see the bibliography), has done Pennsylvanians a great favor by separating the felonious Davey Lewis of fact and tradition, from Davey Lewis, the fabricated felon. As Macneal writes (2011):

> "So many folk legends sprang up about Davey Lewis, the courteous Gentleman Bandit, that folklorists expected him to become a national magnet for local stories. The only factual accounts we have, apart from his dramatic death, were extensive notes (taken) at his trial for counterfeiting in 1816. But he enjoyed a third history, unique to himself—a romantic life story invented by a Carlisle newspaperman who claimed it was Davey's "Confession" from a Bellefonte dungeon.

> "David Lewis was a native of Centre County. Before he was twenty-five he had become Pennsylvania's most colorful highwayman and counterfeiter. All his (adult) life he retired to wilderness hideouts to print money and lay low, from caves near Maryland to the Sinnemahoning frontier in Clinton and Clearfield counties. He never realized that where a stranger is sure to attract attention is where he stands out in an empty landscape. His love of bragging also got him caught many times, giving him a chance to hone his skills as a jailbreaker. Smooth speech and courtly manners earned him the tag of "Robin Hood" many decades before Prince Farrington was so named.

> "In a typical incident he learned of a poor widow who was about to lose her one cow to the tax collector. Lewis lay in wait until the tax collector had taken the cow some distance from her house before robbing him and returning to give the widow enough money to cover her lost cow — keeping a modest profit for himself. A Bellefonte posse caught up with Lewis for the

last time on the Sinnemahoning, wounding and capturing him in a gunfight. Locked up in the Bellefonte jail, he refused to have his wounded arm amputated to save his life and died of gangrene poisoning, barely thirty years old."

JOHN KEHOE (1837 – 1878) ~ Kehoe was an Irishman who came to Pennsylvania to work in the coal mines at a time when mine owners showed no sympathy for the workers. The owners maintained their own police and forbade miners from forming unions. John Kehoe was believed to be the head of a secret miners' group known as the *Molly Maguires*. Some members of the *Molly Maguires* were eventually charged with 16 murders that had occurred during the 1860s and early 1870s. During the years of 1875-77, twenty "Mollies" were hanged; some in Pottsville; some in Mauch Chunk (now Jim Thorpe), some in Bloomsburg and one in Sunbury. John Kehoe, referred to as "King of the Mollies," had gone from mining to operating a bar in Mahanoy City. He was arrested and charged with a murder that had occurred in 1862. Kehoe was convicted in 1877 and was sentenced to hang. An appeal to the governor was denied and, in 1878 he climbed the gallows steps in Pottsville. An overflowing crowd viewed the ghastly procedure in which Kehoe appeared to struggle for twelve minutes before dying. After a wake in Girardville, John Kehoe was buried in a cemetery in Tamaqua. 101 years later, John Kehoe was pardoned by Pennsylvania's governor, Milton J. Shapp.

HARRY LONGABAUGH (1867 – 1908?) ~ Of Pennsylvania renegades, Harry Longabaugh has the *least* familiar name and the *most* familiar name. This seeming paradox arises from the fact that his name from infancy remains utterly unfamiliar. Yet, the name that graced his "Wanted" posters is very familiar.

Harry Longabaugh was born in Mont Clare, just outside Phoenixville in Chester County. He left home as a young teenager and came to be in Wyoming in 1887, where he also came to be imprisoned in a small town's jail as a horse thief. He was pardoned and released in early 1889. Since the Wyoming town in which he had served jail time was named *Sundance*, Longabaugh became known as "The Sundance Kid." Eventually Longabaugh joined the "Hole-in-the-Wall" gang, which was led by another cowboy with an alias, Robert Leroy Parker ("Butch Cassidy"). Butch and Sundance became the subjects of a very popular, Academy Award winning Western film in 1969. The gang robbed banks and trains while the native Pennsylvanian was a member. After several years, Butch and Sundance, along with Sundance's mistress, Etta Place, traveled to Bolivia and other destinations in South America. One account says that Etta returned to the United States, while Butch Cassidy and the Sundance Kid died in a hail of bullets in the Bolivian village of San Vicente. However, the town has no written records or matching graves to support the story. Likewise, no one has ever found conclusive evidence as to the real identity of Etta Place. So, unless more reliable sources are unearthed, Harry Longabaugh will remain a notorious Pennsylvania-born renegade; but with no conclusion to his biography.

Of the above five renegades, two were portrayed in movies by Oscar-winning actors. Sean Connery had the role of John Kehoe and Robert Redford played Longabaugh, "The Sundance Kid."

PRINCE DAVID FARRINGTON (1889 – 1956)

This biography, in two volumes (*Prohibition's Prince* and *Prince and the Paupers*), offers compelling evidence that we have a very fascinating sixth individual to add to our *Keystone State Renegades' Roster*. That individual is Prince David Farrington. Here we have reviewed the second half of his legend.

Once legendary status has been assigned, additional legendary thoughts arise in the fertile fields of our imagination. Consider the suspicion, among some local residents, that the Mile Run Exit to Interstate 80, in Union County, Pennsylvania, was created by some conspiring officials so that one would have easier access to any backwoods stills that might still be cooking hooch in the sylvan darkness of what was once "Farrington Country." Admittedly, that isolated exit, at mile 199 on this great public highway, has no services or nearby population centers. The vivid imagination can almost smell the 'alky' cooking. However, this highway was built more than a decade after the death of Prince Farrington and even more years from the time of his last known moonshining activity. Still, this seemingly God-forsaken interchange is only about five miles from the Tea Spring, where a once-thriving still had been raided before Interstate 80 was built. Even more intriguing, the Mile Run interchange is just about three miles from the Sand Run Lodge, a former farm that was converted into a hunting camp and was owned by well-to-do members and which, coincidentally, was once managed by local moonshiner, Floyd Curtis Klobe. The Sand Run Lodge was there long before Interstate 80 and it is still there today. But, state officials emphasize this: The Mile Run Interchange was created to comply with state guidelines calling for interchanges to be placed so that no excessive stretch of interstate was without access and egress.

Still, suspicions remain. After all, if the isolated, woodland interchange at Mile Run hadn't been built, the unbroken stretch would be a mere 18 miles; the distance from the Carroll interchange (mile 192) to the New Columbia interchange (mile 210).

SLOW TO GAIN MENTION IN LOCAL BOOKS

Despite growing discussion about the presence of Prince Farrington in the Sugar Valley area, writings coming from the valley have been slow to acknowledge his historic presence there. A case in point: The new (2011) book, *Images of Sugar Valley* (see the bibliography), has more than 125 pages, of captioned pictures, with a total of about 225 appealing old photographs of the Loganton/Sugar Valley area. Yet, it is only in the book's introduction that the reader will find one mention, and a fleeting one at that, of the valley's (and the county's) best known historical figure. The full quote, from page 10, states, "Two other well-known Rosecrans residents were Samuel Motter and Prince Farrington. In the second half of the 1800s, Motter gained a reputation as a trapper, fisherman and eccentric adventurer. Farrington was a legendary bootlegger during Prohibition. He purchased a farm at Rosecrans as a cover-up for his stills."

A TOUCHING LEGEND

A story out of rural Lycoming County informs us that Prince Farrington was said to have given one of his last stills to his sons and that they neglected to tear down the still before hunting season opened. The still was spotted by hunters and authorities were notified. Agents then went to the site and blew up that relic.

GAMBLE FARM INN: A HISTORIC 'WAYSIDE INN'

This particular 'wayside inn' is on U.S. Route 220, a bustling highway stretching from the Pennsylvania/New York border, at Waverly, New York, across the entire stretch of Pennsylvania to disappear into Dixie. In Lycoming County, Pennsylvania, it passes just a few hundred yards from the *last domicile* of Prince David Farrington, the *Antiques Inn* (Now known as *The Gamble Farm Inn.*) Ironically, this same U.S. route also passes Prince Farrington's *childhood* home, "Nubbin Ridge," by a mere three miles, before reaching its terminus at the town of Rockingham, North Carolina.

As the writing of this book was entering its last days, a local entrepreneur, named Troy Musser, opened the restored *Gamble Farm Inn* in historic Jersey Shore. This means that what was once the residence of the aging and ailing Prince Farrington (I: 248, etc.) has been handed a vibrant new life. Not only did Musser revitalize the old Inn; but he erected a new motel on the premises. As noted above, the inn-motel complex is very close to an exit on busy U.S. 220. Musser already owns several authentic Farrington relics, including an unopened bottle of Prince's moonshine and one of his bottle-capping machines. The gift shop will feature

Prince Farrington items, just as the dining room will carry a Farrington-themed cuisine. Musser's enterprises are bound to enhance the legend of the once-flamboyant moonshiner.

CHAPTER NINE

Conclusion

The Ballad of Prince Farrington
~ 1889 - 1956 ~

Old Carolina's native son:
Prince Farrington, Prince Farrington.
A lad of sixteen tender years,
When taken from his youthful peers
And placed within a Dixie cell.
Crime gripped him in its lifelong spell.
Soon Pennsylvania's wooded hills
Were hiding his illegal stills.

From Loganton to Antes Fort
And on the Pike to Coudersport;
On hilltop or in swampy sink,
Prince cooked a very potent drink.
For grain, he paid inflated rates
And helped all those in troubled straits.
He bought protection from the law,
So raids were few ~ the ones he saw.

Prince spent his years at moonshine's pail,
Ignoring whiskey's deadly trail.
Drink killed one brother, very young,
Whose ode to life was never sung.
Another brother, daily drunk.
Spouse Martha, often in a funk.
His world left many folks with scars;
His world . . . of barrels, kegs and jars.

Bizarre's the tale I'm telling you;
Yet, all I've told you here is true.
His ling'ring legend has begun.
Prince Farrington, Prince Farrington!

§ **§** §

The early English poet laureate, John Dryden (1631-1700), offered a few lines that suggest that a truly worthy person doesn't require fictitious embellishment.

"Draw him strictly, so
That all who view the piece may know
He needs no trappings of fictitious fame."

The testimonials of many, many individuals remove the need for imaginary tales of Prince Farrington. No matter what the reader's opinion of the man might be, the legitimate praise heaped on Prince Farrington's memory is enough to sustain the opinion that he was a unique member of his community. Before his death in 1956, he was already becoming legendary. The legend remains and grows.

While this biography has concentrated on Prince's two-county area of activity, Clinton and Lycoming counties, Dave Porter, Prince's grandson, says that Prince was also well-known in Penns Valley, another rich agricultural belt in Centre County.

Jim Phoenix is a coach of girls softball at Central Mountain Middle School. During the 1980s he worked at Reading Meats in Flemington. There was, he recalls, a strange individual who walked the streets of Flemington (the town that links Lock Haven and Mill Hall). This man had crutches and a wagon. This man would enter the meat shop and talk of making moonshine. He would ask to buy sugar; but never wanted to buy a full five pounds. He also offered, in return for the granular sweetener, a 'pint' of excellent whiskey. Reading Meats never accepted his offer and never learned the true identity of this stranger, who may or may not have been related to Prince Farrington, Sr. It was simply that those who encountered him, assumed that there must be a connection.

Just as the unidentified stranger who once moved through the streets of Lock Haven on crutches has become part of the legend, the claim attributed to Art Decker fits that description. Decker, of Antes Fort was a lineman for a utility company. But, Art had also claimed to have driven for Prince Farrington and he also claimed, in later years, that there were still caves in which Prince's booze was hidden.

When one learns of the many ways in which Prince Farrington kept secrets from authorities and others, the unproved claim of hidden storage caves or similar caches becomes more convincing. Perhaps that's why Lawrence Lebin, a retired educator from the Mill Hall area, has expressed suspicions that Prince Farrington may not have been 'penniless' as some suggested.

More evidence of a Farrington legend (I: Chapter 11) involved a mention in National Geographic Magazine, several ballads with musical support, many newspaper and magazine articles and, for a decade or so, an annual charity event, *The Prince Farrington Great Race*, in Williamsport.

Admittedly, a neighbor boy, Tom Bauman, was almost like a son to Prince Farrington. Several incidents showed this trait. Here's one. Bauman relates:

> We were still living down there on the farm and there was a guy over in Antes Fort who had something like a little hardware store. He sold seeds, tools, shovels, picks and so on. His name was Newt Thompson. Prince had come down to the house for something. Dad came in and told Mom, "I'm gonna go with Prince. He wants to go over to Antes Fort to the store." I said, "Can I go along?" "Yeah, come on." So, I went out and got in the middle of the front seat. Prince drove us over there. We went into this guy's place. I don't know if you remember: The Case company used to have this display card with all different kinds of pocketknives. Boy! I looked and I really wanted a knife. So, I asked my dad. It wasn't near Christmas or anything like that. It was summertime. "No," he said, "You'll only cut yourself with that... or you'll lose it."
>
> I went out and sat on the porch, 'cause they were still inside shooting the bull. I saw them coming out, so I went and got into the car. They got in the car and Prince backed the car and headed over toward the farm. I felt Prince fiddling at my pocket and reached down; but Prince just took my hand away. Anyhow, we got home and he took us down to the house and we all got out. They had to go to the barn or something. I couldn't wait until they were out of sight. There was that pearl-handled pocket knife! Boy! I didn't say anything to Dad. I had it for quite a long time before Dad ever found out. (Anyhow, if I had that knife today and we carried them the way we did then, we'd get expelled from school!) But, I carried that knife through school and through high school. (In high school his knife was loaned and lost.)

Prince Farrington's charm has been reported in newspapers, as well as in the endless conversations that are still occurring. Mary Lee Troup, of Beaver Springs, in Snyder County, was a native of the Williamsport area. She tells of her mother, as a young woman, being employed, at one time or another, in the offices of one of two Williamsport area companies: The U.S. Rubber Company and the C.A. Reed Company. This was in the 1920s, within the early years of Prince Farrington's residency in Pennsylvania. He was, at that time, aside from his moonshine-making, delivering soft drinks. Ms. Troup's mother related the impression Farrington had on the women, when he stepped into an office, removed his hat and bowed deeply, while saying, in his finest Southern accent, "Good morning, Ladies!" As Mary Lee Troup relates, all the office girls thought Prince to be "quite handsome." Ms. Troup also tells of her parents, as a young couple, knowing the location of a Farrington still site along the old Coudersport Pike. The young couple would walk from the highway into the woods, where they directly bought from the operators, a quantity of Farrington whiskey.

Prohibition, mentioned in Chapter One, gave rise to secret still sites; but it also gave rise to countless secret places where the thirsty could purchase the outlawed alcoholic drinks. The illegal barroom was just one cultural phenomenon born of the Prohibition era. Operating outside the law made barroom owners very careful not to allow strangers to patronize, since the strangers might be law officers, preparing to raid the illicit business. Thus, a potential patron would whisper, or *speak easy*, to the doorman, to gain admission. That precaution led all such secret barrooms to become known as "*speakeasies*." The term, '*speakeasy*,' went out of style in 1933, with the end of Prohibition.

At one time, Prince Farrington operated a *speakeasy* on the old Gheen (now Courtright) farm. ith the passing of Prince's sister, Nade Coltrane, Kyle Coltrane, the widower, and his three children moved in with Prince for a while. B. W., who helped Prince tally his inventory, etc., was especially popular locally; but it was B. W.'s brother, Wade, who married a local girl, Betty Koch.

After the Coltranes vacated the Gheen farmhouse, Prince welcomed the Spong family to be his tenants in the former Gheen house. He engaged the woman, Minnie Spong, an experienced bartender, to manage his speakeasy. Minnie was said to have managed a hotel somewhere, before working for Prince. Also, years later, one of Minnie's daughters was running the Venture Inn a couple of miles north of Jersey Shore on Pine Creek. Prince's personal speakeasy on the Gheen farm offered patrons the opportunity to buy alcoholic drinks, play four or five nickel slot machines and, sometimes, listen to live music. When they departed for the night, customers often took along a supply of liquor for later- perhaps a quart bottle; maybe a gallon jug. Bauman says, "They always had some kind of entertainment." Minnie Spong once hired a regional band to provide some music at the speakeasy. That band had four members and offered customers the sounds of an accordion, a banjo, a guitar and a washboard, the last of which was played by a fellow wearing thimbles.

Tom Bauman's mother, Meda Leah Bauman, wanted to hear the music, so she drove the family's 1929 Chrysler automobile down the lengthy country lane to the Gheen farm. Meda Leah and young Tom enjoyed the musical program. Tom tells us that, at one point, the band's accordion player told the patrons that he was going to sing a song that was a favorite of Prince's. With the small band accompanying, the accordion player then sang (except for occasional humming of some forgotten lyrics) the country hit, "Have You Ever Been Lonely?" That song, composed by Peter De Rose and with lyrics by Billy Hill, was published in 1932 and was first recorded in 1933. The song was especially popular, with recordings by nearly two dozen artists. Such noted singers as Teresa Brewer, Jim Reeves, Jim Ed Brown and Patsy Cline gave voice to the lyrics of apology and regret. However, the recordings of those four singers were all made *after* Prince Farringon's death. The most likely versions to have been heard by Prince Farrington would have been the first one recorded (in 1933, by Ted Mack, a now-nearly forgotten singer) and the 1947 rendering by country star, Ernest Tubb. It would be silly to speculate on whether or not Farrington applied the lyrics to his own broken marriage with Martha White Farrington. Still, the words, excerpted here, fascinate:

> "Oh, be a little forgiving
>   Take me back in your heart.
> How can I go on living,
> Now that we're apart?
> If you knew what I'd been through,
> You'd know why I ask you:
> Have you ever been lonely?
> Have you ever been blue?"

Tom Bauman, of Castanea, has other marvelous recollections of Prince Farrington. Tom's father, Raymond Bauman, another non-drinker who moved among the moonshiners, remained a friend of Prince Farrington throughout his lifetime. The '29 Chrysler that Mrs. Bauman drove to the Gheen Farm speakeasy was part of a pair that was purchased at the same time. The 6-cylinder Chrysler that Tom's father owned was similar in color to the 8-cylinder, 1929 Chrysler that Prince got. Tom says that Prince's fine, new machine was purchased with a proper mix of cash and liquor.

Few living people have more than a memory or two of having encountered Prince David Farrington. For the boy, Tom Bauman, encountering his neighbor, Prince Farrington, was almost commonplace and certainly wasn't limited to the time that Prince bought him a pearl-handled pocket knife.

Positive opinions of Prince were also commonplace. For example, Tom Bauman's wife, Geneva Goodman Bauman, a lifelong resident of Castanea, states emphatically, that Prince Farrington "was a good man." And, she adds that his family members were also good people. Her husband gained a similar opinion from regular contact with Prince and his family members, as mentioned in the first chapter. However, Tom Bauman had several additional encounters to recall.

Young Bauman was with Prince and Whitey on a trip to Jersey Shore. There, Prince and Tom Bauman waited in the car for Whitey to get his hair cut. While the bootlegger and the farmer's son were waiting, Prince asked, "How is your dad? I haven't seen him for awhile." Then, "Your Mom?" When Tom Bauman acknowledged that they were alright, Prince followed with, "I want to tell you something. Your dad is the only person that ever worked for me, that never tried to take me. He's as honest as the day is long."

The raid, about 1932 of Prince's place was a chaotic time for the Baumans (two parents and three children). Tom remembers the raid as being like a circus. It lasted through two days and a night. Local people were rushing to see and, if possible, to sop (gathering as much of the spilled liquor as they could get before it sank into the ground or flowed into the river). Since the authorities made little effort to keep spectators away, they accumulated to enjoy the spectacle. After all, how many people are lucky enough to witness a genuine revenue agents' raid? Bauman muses about the crowd. "Every drunk in Lycoming County, I think, was down there."

At Prince's neighbors' farm, the Baumans saw their cellar steps removed so that the officials could create a makeshift setup for getting whiskey kegs up from the cellar. They were then rolled downhill, while an agent stood on each side and tried to smash open the two ends with sledgehammers. Not every barrel end broke; but some that did still held some of the valuable moonshine.

Even then, when the raid finally ended, the Baumans found a barrel in the cellar that hadn't been removed or smashed. Their maternal uncle, Floyd Shaffer, salvaged that last full barrel and sold it to Joe Gardner. It was worth, by the gallon, nearly $500.00. All the moonshine that had been on the Bauman farm had been aging for about five years, which made the loss was even more painful. Agents had checked the tractor shed, silo and just about everywhere imaginable; but had found no more booze. Then, when it seemed that their portion of the raid was completed, one of the agents decided to drive a 3/8 inch piece of metal pipe into the haw mow. "Thump." The hay had been covering a huge, and valuable, stash; now destined to flow into the Susquehanna, from which no revenue would ever flow back in return. Yet, despite the agents likely finding over a hundred kegs and barrels of moonshine, in their several hiding places, the Baumans were only questioned; but not arrested.

When Floyd Shaffer and Prince Farrington were in Lewisburg, Floyd's sisters, including Tom's mother, took Tom and drove to the penitentiary. Although Tom was not allowed to any inmate, his mother and aunts got to speak with Floyd, but were denied visiting privileges with Prince.

Another time, authorities came to Prince's house. While searching, they ran across a bill that was lying on Prince's desk. A local individual had submitted the invoice to Prince for payment. The bill showed that Prince had hired the man to set up a still. That bill incriminated Prince, who was saddled with an eleven-month prison sentence in the Lewisburg penitentiary. Tom's uncle, Floyd Shaffer, who had set up the still and who had submitted the bill, earned a nine-month stay in the same walled facility as his employer.

A CLUSTER OF POSITIVE TRAITS

Prince David Farrington had so little formal education that he barely got through the first eight grades. Yet, he was a skilled welder, a knowledgeable farmer, an impressive dresser, a natural diplomat, an astute businessman and an expert distiller. Farrington possessed considerable common sense and a coolness under pressure. For observing Prince Farrington's best traits, one need only review his many encounters with his neighbor, Tom Bauman. Bauman didn't simply observe numerous positive traits of the master moonshiner. He was the beneficiary of several.

Another major incident involving Bauman and Prince Farrington, reveals several of Prince's personal qualities at once. Tom narrates a very different, and very personal, story. He tells of working with Prince and Prince's youngest son, Whitey. "There was a field," Bauman relates, "out there, right below the (Antes Fort – Jersey Shore) airport. Prince and Whitey had taught me how to drive their Ford tractor. So they were at the barn on the Gheen farm, getting ready to plant soy beans, while I was plowing. If it (an incident) had happened at any other time, I might have lost a leg or something.

"Anyhow, I'd just started down along the old fence row, trying to plow all the land that I could. I was driving the Ford tractor, which had hydraulic lift. Just as I picked up the plows, the left front wheel caught a fence post that was hanging out on its wire! It jerked the steering wheel out of my hand. As I reached to grab the wheel, my foot slipped down and right under the right tire! Luckily, I had the throttle (speed control) back and it stalled the tractor; but it stalled it right on my leg! There I was. I started screaming like a wild Indian!

"There was an old, one-room schoolhouse down at the end of that field and earlier I had seen these guys at the old schoolhouse, fiddling around with furniture or something. I started hollering like hell! Anyhow, I didn't know this; but Whitey and Prince had come out the road in their pickup truck. They stopped to wait for me; then decided that I must be plowing another round. They sat there for a little bit, waiting. Then Prince asked, 'Whitey, isn't that Tom hollering?' Whitey said, 'Yeah!' so they came tearing down over that unplowed ground in the Ford truck. I thought they were flying! When they pulled out onto the plowed ground, the truck stalled!

"They bailed out of the truck and ran over to me. Whitey jumped on the tractor and was going to try backing it off of me; but Prince said, 'Don't! You might spin the wheel on his leg!' They, too, had seen the guys at that building, so Whitey ran down through that field... it must have been two or three hundred yards down there, and he was out of breath when he got there. Those guys asked Whitey, 'What's the matter?' Whitey said, 'My buddy's under the tractor up there!'

"Meanwhile, Prince got under that wheel... and he was strong! Nobody will ever tell me that he wasn't extra strong! Prince pulled up and he held as much of that weight off my leg as he could. Then he slipped, you know, and he'd have to let it down again... and I'd moan a little bit more.
Finally, here comes Whitey and those guys in that old Chevy car and they all jumped out and jumped over the fence. They all got hold and pushed the tractor off of me.

"Prince reached down and picked me up just like I was a baby. When he picked me up, I said, 'I'm alright, Prince. I'm alright. Just let me down.' Prince let me down; but he held on to me till I walked around a little bit.

"The wheel on my leg had shut the blood flow in my leg and I also had the tire track bruise right down that leg, you know. Also, the tractor had wooden pegs where you rested our feet. When I slipped off the side, those pegs tore my pant leg and bruised the *inside* of my leg. I often thought about that. If that tractor hadn't stalled and would have kept going, with those plows up in the air, they probably would have slammed right into me!"

Tom Bauman stayed at the Gheen house until the circulation returned and he could walk comfortably. When Raymond Bauman arrived to take his son home,

Prince told him what had happened. "It wasn't Tom's fault," Prince declared. "That damned fencepost, hanging out on that wire, just jerked the steering wheel out of his hand." Tom assures us that his dad still liked the Ford brand of tractor. He says that, just a year after that accident, Raymond Bauman bought his first Ford tractor, off "Doc" Derk in Jersey Shore ("Doc" was a car dealer; but he was also a veterinarian). Over the years, Raymond Bauman had a total of four Ford tractors.

Amid people's negative and positive recollections of Prince Farrington, a few stand out. Another couple of Tom Bauman's positive remembrances must be offered here so that this, the second half of Farrington's biography can end on a positive; yes, on a *very* positive note.

Tom relates that, when he was about five years old, his mother ordered a shepherd dog for him. It was ordered from a place in Wisconsin. He had that dog for 16 years, until it died when he was a senior in high school. The shepherd dog was purchased because Tom had already been given a police dog; but his mother had read about a police dog maiming a boy, so she asked the gift giver to take it back. The man who graciously accepted the police dog's return was the Bauman's generous neighbor, Prince David Farrington, Sr.

Another interaction between Tom Bauman's and his moonshiner neighbor, in Tom's own words:

> "Prince was like a favorite uncle to me. He gave me the first gun I ever owned. Dad and I were visiting down there one time. Whitey Farrington had this Benjamin air rifle. You pumped it up and it shot 22 caliber pellets. Well, Whitey had shot some windows out of the garage or something. So, when Dad and I were going out to get in the car, Prince reached in the corner and said, 'Here'," and handed me the rifle.

> "With that air rifle, I shot a good many rats and pigeons in our barn. The damned pigeons would shit on our equipment. My dad would try to keep the barn closed; but those pigeons would always find a way in, you know. My dad was a stickler for putting equipment inside when you're done with it; not so much the harrows; but we had binders, corn planters, a mower. They had to be inside. He didn't want them rusting. That's where my gun helped. I could shoot my Benjamin air rifle in the barn. My brother had a single-shot 22-gauge rifle. I wouldn't dare shoot that in the barn because it would blow holes out through the roof!

> "After I'd come home from military service, I was working for my uncle. This was about 1946 or 1947, about the time that Prince had a still up on the Scootac. (Tangascootac Creek). We were doing work up near the Jersey

Shore High School. As I was going up on Church Street, I passed a garage and saw Prince putting gas in his one-half-ton pick-up truck. I parked my truck and got out. We shook hands and I said, 'I haven't seen you....' We exchanged greetings. It was the last time I ever saw Prince."

Tom Bauman, who used no alcohol, expressed only positive thoughts about America's top moonshiner. Let's conclude the Bauman praise with one clear quote: "You know, in all the time that I knew Prince, I never heard anybody say anything bad about him."

As was stated before (I: 76), Prince Farrington made sure that local children attending the Lycoming County Fair had some money available. He also sent barefoot children to a Jersey Shore shoe store where he kept an open account. He was also remembered for having first graders start their educational journey with a new pair of jeans, a new shirt and a new pair of shoes.

VOICES IN THE WILDERNESS

The evidence is clear: Prince David Farrington was highly regarded among his friends and neighbors. The positive remarks made about the man far outnumbered the negative statements. However, we would be remiss if we neglected to present the thoughts expressed by people who did not appreciate whatever it was that Farrington was doing for the community.

In *Prohibition's Prince*, we quoted at least one individual critic as well as a forceful statement, in a newspaper (I: 199), regarding respect for the law and the sort of society we would have if everyone took the attitude of Prince Farrington. Individuals did complain. They may have been in the minority in the area; but let's hear their voices.

David Doerr's family moved into Sugar Valley in 1870. They lived in the area east of Loganton, near the Price Cemetery. That cemetery once was attached to the Price Evangelical Church; but the church had a small congregation and eventually offered only monthly services. The Doerr family tale tells us that there was only crawl space beneath the church; but Prince Farrington hid whiskey in the crawl space. As a teen, Robert Doerr was given $5.00 by Prince Farrington to watch the stash and let Prince know if it was disturbed. Some felt that Prince increased his acceptance in the community by giving money for some exaggerated, or imaginary, needs. In any case, young Robert Doerr used his money to buy a bicycle. He could now ride his bike the three and one-half miles to school. Sadly, he soon had a cycling accident that broke his arm.

Later, Robert Doerr became a binge drinker and his aunt was quick to let the community know that her sottish nephew was given his first drink by Prince Farrington.

As an aside, we might mention Charles Womeldorf, who also lived east of Loganton, was said to have made his own booze in the 1950's and sold some of it. In fact, Robert Doerr's spinster sister, Eleanor, later converted Womeldorf's mash tubs into handy planters and used them for growing flowers.

Marjorie Kamus, (I: 159-160, etc.), of Jersey Shore, is unsparing in her criticism of Prince Farrington. Regarding his fame, she now observes: "It wasn't a good famous. It was an 'Al Capone' famous, except that Prince didn't carry a gun. He was good to people because he needed drivers and other people to run the stills and so on." In more recent years, Marjorie, herself, has owned the store across the highway from the old paint mill on Antes Creek. She also recalls accompanying her dad on a visit to Colonel Henry Shoemaker's home in order to see the author's antiques. Why? Because, she tells us, "people did things that didn't cost a lot of money."

Another individual who heard some unvarnished criticism of Prince Farrington was Phil Ferrar. Phil's grandfather, Edward (Joseph Edward Ferrar) worked for Prince. 'Edward' Feerrar told Phil that he had been a runner for Prince and recalled taking Farrington alcohol to Washington, D.C. for delivery to several people, including the U.S. president. However, Phil expresses some doubt about the claims of his grandfather, since Edward "had a huge drinking problem in his middle years." Phil Feerar notes that his "siblings blamed his relationship with Prince as leading to the destruction of his marriage and to his losing his faculties." Phil Feerrar concludes that, "growing up I was taught Prince was a felon, not someone to admire."

MORE PLAUDITS FOR PRINCE

Another neighbor, John Muthler, lived on the neighboring farm when Prince Farrington lived near Antes Fort. Muthler, whose own family did not use alcohol, says that he never saw Prince drunk and that he was "Always dressed in a suit." That was before Prince's stay in the Federal penitentiary in Lewisburg. After his release, however, Muthler says that Prince was normally dressed as a dirt farmer.

Bernard Wynn, whose grandfather worked for Prince, suggests that his great aunt would have considered Prince Farrington to be "a common crook," but, Wynn declares, "In my (immediate) family, you really didn't say anything bad about him."

Harold Adams is a retired educator who was born and raised in Sugar Valley. He offered this summary of Prince's reputation in Sugar Valley:

> "When Prince Farrington had the Florida Fruit Farm, if farmers had trouble selling their crops, they could sell them to Prince. Prince always kind of looked out for the people over there. And to this day, you can't say anything bad about Prince Farrington in Sugar Valley. If you do, you're going to get an argument. That's the way it was. He was well-liked."

THE TIME FACTOR

If we want to learn of the reaction to Prince David Farrington in the two primary counties involved in his wildly colorful career, we must align events of his life with the calendar.

When Prince first arrived in Pennsylvania, the reception would have been mixed. Those who wanted a source of alcohol would have been pleased to make his acquaintance. Still, a large number, likely more than half, might have said, "The last thing we need around here is another person pushing alcohol!" The longer he was here, the smaller that chorus would have become. As his supply of moonshine increased, his appreciative customers would have grown in quantity. Finally, even though the institution of prohibition was ending, larger numbers of local people would have been impressed with the wealth he continued to generate and to share. The sentiment would likely have been something like, "The main thing that we need around here is someone with money to spend!" Prince Farrington's influence may have increased steadily until his last arrest. Once Farrington's presence was lacking, his importance waned.

SIX TO STAY IN SHANGRI-LA

James Hilton (1900-1954) was an English novelist. His one book, *Lost Horizon* (1933) told of a fabulous land, lost in a mountain range, where most residents barely aged. The name of that fictitious land gave us a name for any place that borders on the idyllic: *Shangri-La*. For Prince and his Tarheel friends, that might have been Clinton/Lycoming counties in Pennsylvania. Perhaps it's the friendly people. Possibly it's the air. Or maybe it's the magnificent scenery. We can't know. What we do know is that Prince, his brother Charl, Colonel Segraves, Joe Gardner, George Gardner and Lemuel Groce all came from rural North Carolina to make a little liquor in Pennsylvania, and all six remained for the rest of their lives in the Keystone State. So far as we can determine, all but Prince are buried here,

141

as well. Clearly, this sextet of moonshiners and neighbors became forever attached to the land and the people of Pennsylvania.

FULLER'S FRANK EVALUATION

Despite a sometimes reluctant welcome from his relatives around *Nubbin Ridge*, Prince Farrington did return home for visits. One never knew if he was drawn south by real family ties or by something related to his moonshining occupation. However, one visit seems to have been clearly motivated by family ties. Sam Fuller, who did considerable driving for Prince, including that of chauffeur, remembered the trip during which he drove one of several trucks that Prince was delivering to Oklahoma City, Oklahoma. On the return trip, Sam and Prince came through North Carolina where they spent three weeks visiting at Prince's old homestead. Fuller, now in his 80s and filled with rich memories, remains active and gets to South Williamsport to attend weekly dances. Sam Fuller also offered this very succinct observation about Prince Farrington: "He was a helluva nice guy!"

The principal characters who graced the pages of this book have left many, many descendants to carry their names or their blood lines into future generations. One example: When Ida Stabley died, in 1959, a local newspaper noted that she had 65 descendants. That number should exceed 100 in 2011. A second example: Herman Henry and Margaret Miller Klobe had two sons and a daughter, Charles, Floyd and Mildred. Those three had, respectively, eleven children, one child and one child. That baker's dozen of grandchildren of Herman and Margaret Klobe has now swelled to more than a hundred descendants! Similarly, Wesley Koch and his wife, Emma, had 11 children, a number that generated many dozens of descendants. Lastly, Prince sired four children with Mattie, while his brother, Charl and his sister-in-law, Virgie, had seven children. Although an accurate count of offspring might not be possible, a tally of descendants for Pennsylvania's two Farrington brothers, numbering in the dozens, is surely valid.

The Farrington legend is daily nourished by the presence of many area residents through whose arteries the diluted blood of a moonshiner pulses. A widening pool of descendants inhabit what was once "Farrington Country." Today, countless area citizens can trace their lineage back to the local moonshiners. They cling to a growing cluster of legends about the colorful days of Coltrane, Farrington, Gardner, Groce, Klobe, Koch, Kohberger, Rockey, Segraves, Seyler and Yarrison, plus the dozens of lesser players. The moonshiners' local offspring, as well as many other enthusiastic local citizens, will insure that the legends thrive and that they are lovingly carried into the countless tomorrows.

BIBLIOGRAPHY

BOOKS

Day, Savannah Segraves, *The Reverend William Segraves and His Descendants*, Pocohantas Press, 1989

Holy Bible, Scofield, C. I., D.D., editor, 1967 edition.

Kagan, David Ira and John W. Harbach, Sr., *Images of America: Sugar Valley Villages*, 2011

The Oxford Universal Dictionary, 3rd edition, 1955

Welshans, Wayne O., *Images of America: Jersey Shore*, 2006

Welshans, Wayne O., *Images of America: Nippenose Valley*, 2008

BOOKLETS

Huddy, Stephen C., and Paul C. Metzger, *Alvira and the Ordnance,* Montgomery Area Historical Society (Montgomery, PA), 2009

How To Make It, No author listed. Marked as being published by the Canadian Publishing Company of Washington Avenue, Philadelphia, Penna. (undated)

PERIODICALS

Macneal, Douglas, *Centre County Heritage*, Vol. 24; Number 2, Fall, 1987. (This entire issue is devoted to the story of David Lewis.)

THE SNYDER COUNTY HISTORICAL SOCIETY BULLETIN, 1996
NEWSWEEK, 11/6/67

TIME, 11/3/67

NEWSPAPERS

Lock Haven Express, LockHaven, PA, several issues

Renovo Record, Renovo, PA, several issues

Sun-Gazette Williamsport, PA, several issues

Wellsboro Agitator, Wellsboro, PA, 8/18/1956

Williamsport Gazette and Bulletin, 1/28/1948

BLOG SITE

http://thepennsylvaniarambler.blogspot.com/search/label/Henry%20Shoemaker, 9/4/11

WEB SITES

Wilson, Ellen, A Passion for the Past
http://www.carnegiemuseums.org/cmag/bk_issue/1996/julaug/dept5.htm
    9/3/11

http://genforum.genealogy.com/shoemaker/messages/747.html 9/3/11

http://phmc.state.pa.us/bah/dam/mg/mg114.htm 9/3/11

http://www.psu.edu/ur/about/myths.html, 9/4/11

http://www.psupress.org/books/titles/0-271-01486-5.html 9/3/11

https://mail.google.com/mail/h/lqzx04qdsvied/?
    &v=c&smi=13293622295c14e1#m_1329...

INDEX